KEY FACTS

EUROPEAN
LAW

CHRIS TURNER

Hodder & Stoughton

A MEMBER OF THE HODDER HEADLINE GROUP

A0038843
£4.99
18/4 12
340.94

Orders: please contact Bookpoint Ltd, 78 Milton Park, Abingdon, Oxon OX14 4TD.
Telephone: (44) 01235 827720. Fax: (44) 01235 400454. Lines are open from 9.00–6.00,
Monday to Saturday, with a 24-hour message answering service.
Email address: orders@bookpoint.co.uk

British Library Cataloguing in Publication Data
A catalogue record for this title is available from The British Library.

ISBN 0 340 845848

First published 2002
Impression number   10 9 8 7 6 5 4 3 2 1
Year   2005 2004 2003 2002

Cover design by Stewart Larking
Typeset by Transet Limited, Coventry, England.
Printed in Great Britain for Hodder & Stoughton Educational, a division of
Hodder Headline Ltd, 338 Euston Road, London NW1 3BH by **Cox & Wyman Ltd, Reading, Berks.**

CONTENTS

PREFACE

The Key Facts series is a practical and complete revision aid that can be used by students of law courses at all levels from A Level to degree and beyond, and in professional and vocational courses.

The Key Facts series is designed to give a clear view of each subject. This will be useful to students when tackling new topics and is invaluable as a revision aid. Most chapters open with an outline in diagram form of the points covered in that chapter. The points are then developed in a structured list form to make learning easier. Supporting cases are given throughout by name and for some complex areas facts are given to reinforce the point being made.

The Key Facts series aims to accommodate the syllabus content of most qualifications in a subject area, using many visual learning aids.

European Law is now a core subject in all qualifying law degrees. It is also a vital subject in which to gain a good understanding since so many other areas of law now are affected by it. It would be difficult to teach or study, for instance, Contract Law, Employment Law, Company Law, or Consumer Law without a reasonable appreciation of the effects of European Law.

The topics covered in *Key Facts: European Law* include all of the main areas of all mainstream syllabuses. When it is studied in the context of the substantive law, European Law is actually a very exiting and developing area of law.

A Table identifying the different numbering of Treaty Articles prior to the Treaty of Amsterdam is included at the end of the book.

The law is as I believe it to be on 1st December 2001.

CHAPTER 1

THE CONSTITUTION AND CHARACTER OF EC LAW

1.1 ORIGINS AND BACKGROUND

1.1.1 The concept of a single Europe

1. The UK tends towards 'euro-scepticism', so two misconceptions usualy prevail:
- that the idea of a united Europe is new;
- that the Community legal order is a haphazard process of co-operation between member states.

2. The Roman Empire is one possible starting point, with several subsequent attempts at European unity or aspirations towards it:
- Papal view of 'Christendom';
- Charlemagne's 'Holy Roman Empire';
- Henry IV of France and the 'Christian Commonwealth of Europe';
- and even the aspirations of Napoleon and Hitler;
- European unity has also been a common theme of every major political philosopher, e.g. Kant, Rousseau, Neitzsche, Marx.

3. So history possibly favours the 'europhiles', with 'euro-scepticism' a more recent nationalist hostility to the EC.

4. Ironically, a federal Europe originated as a British idea.

5. The intellectual architect of 'Europe' was Jean Monnet.

1.1.2 The background to the European Community

1. There have been various attempts at integration in the 19th and 20th centuries.

2. These have been based on need to avoid war, particularly after WW2.

3. There were two key factors:
   - the Treaty of Versailles failed and led to rise of Nazism;
   - so it was vital to bring Germany within the European 'partnership'.
4. Churchill, in his 1947 Zurich speech, said 'We must build a kind of United States of Europe'.
5. The European Union of Federalists was established in 1947.
6. Continental advocates of union argued for 'supranational bodies' in the Montreux Resolution 1947.
7. Various intergovernmental agreements created new world or European organisations at this time: IMF; GATT; OEEC; The Council of Europe; Benelux Union.

1.1.3 The creation of the Treaties

1. The Treaties began with 'Marshall plan' and then 'Schuman plan':
   - the narrow aspect was placing French and German coal and steel production under a 'higher authority';
   - the wider agenda was to move towards a federal Europe.
2. The plan led to the first Treaty: European Coal and Steel Community Treaty (ECSC Treaty) – Treaty of Paris 1951.
   - It also devised an institutional framework of communities (later to be added to by European Court of Justice).
   - Monnet was made first president of ECSC.
3. This was followed by an unsuccessful initiative to create a European Defence Community.
4. Further integration and a move towards the establishment of supranational institutions came with the two Treaties of Rome 1957 – The European Atomic Energy Community Treaty (EURATOM), and The European Economic Community Treaty (EC Treaty).
5. The latter resulted from the 'Spaak Committee Report' and a recommendation for the creation of a 'common market'.
6. The Treaties were originally only signed by six countries: France, Italy, Germany, Belgium, Netherlands, and Luxembourg.

- Different countries had different things to gain.
- This meant that integration was always dogged by national self-interest.
- This ensured that development would be 'incremental' and that principle would be sacrificed to pragmatism.
- As a result, the UK stayed out.

7. Objectives of the Treaties were to be achieved by two means:
   - the creation of a common market and common policies;
   - monetary union.
8. The former has always predominated and dictated the character of the Community.
9. So, the establishment of the 'four freedoms', the removal of internal barriers and, more importantly, the new legal order were required.

1.2 THE DEVELOPMENT OF THE TREATIES (FROM EC, ECSC, EURATOM, TO SEA, TEU, TOA AND TON)

1. The original Treaties have been supplemented and modified, firstly within the Community and then in an evolving Union.
2. The early years of the Community, from 1958 to 1965, were characterised by economic boom:
   - good progress was made towards the creation of a 'customs union', i.e. dismantling of tariffs;
   - but there was far less progress towards an actual common market;
   - some competition policy was put in place;
   - some moves were made towards free movement of workers;
   - but there was over-prominence of the Common Agricultural Policy (CAP);
   - good work was done by the European Court of Justice (ECJ) in defining the character of the legal order.
3. The Common Market should have been achieved within the 'transitional period', i.e. 12 years from 1957, in three four-year periods.

4. However, in 1965–66 DeGaulle created a crisis over qualified majority voting, with France withdrawing from participation in the Council.

5. This was partly resolved by the Luxembourg Accords, which effectively created a sort of veto for member states on major issues (of uncertain future with commitment to integration in the Treaty on European Union).

6. In many ways the years from then until 1986 and the adoption of the Single European Act are seen as years of stagnation in terms of integration.
   - This can partly be explained by economic recession and the retreat into national interest (particularly the UK).
   - However, in other areas the community did develop:
     (i) by enlargement (firstly to 12, then to 15 countries);
     (ii) by broadening (developing policy in and outside the original Treaty objectives – although some took some time to be fully adopted because of national self-interest, e.g. Social Charter);
     (iii) judicial activism of the ECJ (in defining supremacy and developing direct effect and its alternatives).

7. The effective 're-launch' of the Community came in 1986.

8. There were three principal reasons for this:
   - the Commission presidency of Jacques Delors;
   - a commitment to further integration by key political figures in the member states (notably Chancellor Kohl in Germany and President Mitterand in France);
   - the growing realisation that survival depended on an effective EC;
   - the adoption of the Single European Act (with a set time scale of 1992 for implementation of the single market).

9. SEA 1986 included five major provisions:
   - a definition of the internal market and the 1992 deadline;
   - a new law-making process in co-operation with Parliament on certain measures;
   - creation of the Court of First Instance to support the ECJ;
   - provision for compulsory rather than *ad hoc* meetings of a European Council twice yearly (formally recognised);

- the idea of European Political Co-operation.

10. Treaty on European Union (TEU) (signed at Maastricht) followed in 1992.
    - It did not include everything most states wanted.
    - The UK was allowed to opt out of the most important parts in order to secure a treaty at all.
    - So the desired environmental laws were not included.
    - There was only agreement to co-operate on defence and justice, rather than being part of the legal order.
    - Eleven of the then 12 agreed on the Social Chapter, but the UK opted out, thus necessitating the protocol procedure.
    - But it did create the union and the idea of European citizenship – though not within the legal order.

11. The Treaty of Amsterdam 1997 then re-numbered the Articles of the EC Treaty, and the UK signed the Social Chapter.

12. The Treaty of Nice creates planned changes to the composition of the institutions, voting procedures, enlargement, and 'enhanced cooperation'.

1.3 BASIC AIMS AND OBJECTIVES OF EC LAW AND SUPRANATIONALISM

1. The objectives of the EC are quite simply stated in the EC Treaty, as amended and built on by later Treaties: 'to promote throughout the community a harmonious development of economic activities, a continuous, balanced expansion, an increase in stability, an accelerated raising of the standard of living and quality of life and closer relations between the states belonging to it and sustainable development of economic activities, a high level of employment and of social protection, equality between men and women, sustainable and non-inflationary growth, a high degree of competitiveness and convergence of economic performance, a high level of protection and of improvement of the quality of the environment, and economic and social cohesion among the member states.'

2. It is easy to assume that the constitution of the EC is no more than what is laid down in the Treaties, but this would be only partly true because all constitutions are defined by how they are interpreted in the Courts.

3. The EC constitution has the added complication of being founded in Treaty relationships entered into by sovereign states.

4. So, the first problem is identifying how Treaties come to be incorporated in Member States' law. There are two approaches:
   - Monist constitutions – these include France and the Netherlands. The Treaty is automatically incorporated into the national legal system at the point of ratification.
   - Duellist constitutions – these include Germany, Italy, Belgium and, of course, the UK where the Treaty is only incorporated after enactment. (In the UK this was by the European Communities Act 1972.)

5. The result can be a wide variance in how the Treaties are interpreted and applied.

6. In order for the legal order of the Community to function, the institutions must be 'supranational', i.e. in relation to those things covered by the Treaties, they take precedence over national institutions.

7. The ECJ, in administering and defining EC law, and the principle of 'supranationalism' then both become vital to the role of ensuring the universal application of the Treaties:
   - 'To avoid disparities arising out of different national approaches to the incorporation of EC law and to ensure uniformity in its application, the Court of Justice has developed its own jurisprudence on the Supremacy of EC law.' (Penelope Kent: *The Law of the European Union*, Longman)
   - 'ECJ has uniformly and consistently been the most effective integration institution in the Community. Its role was established in (A220) A164: "The Court shall ensure that in the interpretation and application of this Treaty the law is observed." From its very inception in the Treaty, the

ECJ set about establishing its hierarchical authority as the ultimate court of constitutional review. In this area two areas in particular are important. First there is the role of the ECJ in controlling member state courts, and, second, there is the role of the Court in managing the incessant inter-institutional struggles.' (Ian Ward: *A Critical Introduction to European Law*, Butterworths)

8. In respect of the former of these two – defining the relationship between the Community legal order and the member states – three crucial factors apply:
   - the doctrine of Supremacy (or Primacy) of EC law;
   - the A234 reference procedure;
   - the doctrine of direct effect.
9. More recently, indirect effect and state liability have also been developed by the ECJ to ensure that citizens can enforce their rights.

1.4 THE EUROPEAN UNION

1.4.1 General

1. The European Union finally came into force in 1993, only after ratification of the TEU by member states.
2. The TEU created an entirely new structure, over and above that of the EC.
3. The constitution is described as the 'three pillars':
   - Pillar 1: comprises the legal order of the original Treaties, added to by economic and monetary union – so the other pillars are outside the scope of the legal order.
   - Pillar 2: co-operation towards common foreign and security policy.
   - Pillar 3: co-operation towards common systems on justice and home affairs.
4. Pillars 2 and 3 are found in Titles V and VI and not specifically incorporated into UK law.
5. There is debate over whether it is accurate to speak of EU law rather than EC law. Since the two extra pillars created by

TEU have no foundation in law but are based on co-operation, and since the law stems from the EC Treaty not the TEU, it is probably most accurate to use EC to refer to law, and EU to refer to the geographical unit formed by the 15 states.

1.4.2 The institutions of the Union

1. Strictly speaking there are no institutions of the EU.
2. Article 3 of TEU provides that 'The Union shall be served by a single institutional framework ...'
3. Article 5 TEU then says, 'Parliament, the Council, the Commission, and the Court of Justice shall exercise their powers ... for the purposes provided ... on the one hand by the Treaties establishing the Communities ... and on the other hand by the other provisions of this Treaty...'.
4. So the Union 'borrows' the Community's institutions for its own purposes – the fulfillment of the other two pillars.
5. The European Council, however, is extremely significant to the development of the Union.

1.4.3 The objectives of the Union

1. The objectives of the original Treaties have been modified and amended over time by SEA and then TEU.
2. The prime objective of the Union is to achieve the objectives of the Community.
3. But the Union also has added objectives:
   - closer co-operation on justice and home affairs;
   - promotion of social and economic progress which is balanced and sustainable by removing internal frontiers, strengthening economic and social cohesion, and establishing economic and monetary union (with single currency);
   - asserting international identity through common foreign and security policies (including defence policy);

- strengthening protection of rights and interests of nationals through introduction of citizenship;
- maintaining and building upon the *acquis communautaire*.

1.4.4 Decision making/political control in the Union

1. The major power is the Council – has autonomy – little input from other institutions.
2. Commission is said to be 'fully associated' but has no power.
3. The Council has power to take decisions on Titles V and VI, but with little internal effect, so is usually backed up by ratification in member states.
4. Parliament has no influence on Titles V and VI.
5. The ECJ has no jurisdiction either.
6. However, the Union has no provisions like A310 EC Treaty, so external bodies have to deal with either the Community or individual member states.

1.4.5 Common foreign and security policies (Pillar 2)

1. Contained in Title V, Article 13
2. Basic objectives are to 'safeguard common values, fundamental interests and independence of the Union, to strengthen security, preserve peace and develop and consolidate democracy and the rule of law and respect for human rights and fundamental freedoms…'.
3. So, there is a general obligation on member states of 'loyalty and mutual solidarity and to refrain from any action contrary to those objectives'.
4. So there is a general obligation to consult.
5. The Council can decide when a 'common position' is necessary and also when joint action should be taken.

1.4.6 Justice and home affairs (the third pillar)

1. This is contained in Title VI – Article 35.
2. Now, following TOA, the third pillar has been renamed 'Police and Judicial Co-operation in Criminal Matters'.
3. This is controversial because it concerns sensitive issues, e.g. immigration and asylum seeking, judicial and police co-operation, security etc.
4. So it focuses on co-operation, with no mention of implementing policy – although some aspects of the third pillar are now subject to ECJ jurisdiction.
5. Member states have the last say when the Council does reach unanimous decisions on common action.

1.4.7 Final provisions of the TEU

1. The EC Treaty provides simple mechanisms for amending certain issues.
2. Now, other amendments must be made through TEU procedure:
   - the Commission or member state submits an amendment to the Council;
   - the Council decides to hold an intergovernmental conference after consulting with the Commission and Parliament;
   - a unanimous vote in the conference results in the amendment being sent to member states for ratification.
3. Accession must now be to both Union and Community:
   - applications require unanimous approval of Council and assent of Parliament;
   - current applications for membership include Cyprus, Czech Republic, Hungary, Poland, Estonia, Slovenia, Malta, Bulgaria, Latvia, Lithuania, Romania, the Slovak Republic and Turkey;
   - the Commission has stated that applicants fulfilling the necessary criteria should be eligible for entry after 2002 –

Turkey's application is unlikely to succeed at present because of its human rights record.

4. As in the EC Treaty, there is no mention of secession, and there are no mechanisms for withdrawal, which contradicts the UK's position on Parliamentary supremacy.

1.4.8 Some Criticisms of the TEU

1. The UK reduced the scope of the Treaty by opting out of almost all the positive parts.
2. This led to fragmentation and the creation of various protocols, described by some commentators as having no basis in the legal order.
3. So, Maastricht was a surrender to national interests, e.g. subsidiarity, but this seems contradictory as Union is a concept that implies a federal system.
4. The 'democratic deficit' was increased, not decreased:
   - the Commission is still powerful, and still undemocratic;
   - Parliament is increasingly democratic, but still relatively ineffective;
   - the Council is still the major power;
   - so supranationalism was once again sacrificed for national interests.

Common foreign and security policies (Pillar 2) – In Title V	The three Communities – as amended by TEU (Pillar 1), enforceable because a legal order			Police and judicial co-operation in criminal matters (Pillar 3) – in Title VI
	ECSC European Coal and Steel	EC European	EURATOM European Atomic Energy	
	C O M M U N I T Y	C O M M U N I T Y	C O M M U N I T Y	
Based on co-operation				Based on co-operation

The three-pillar structure of the European Union

CHAPTER 2

THE INSTITUTIONS OF THE EUROPEAN UNION

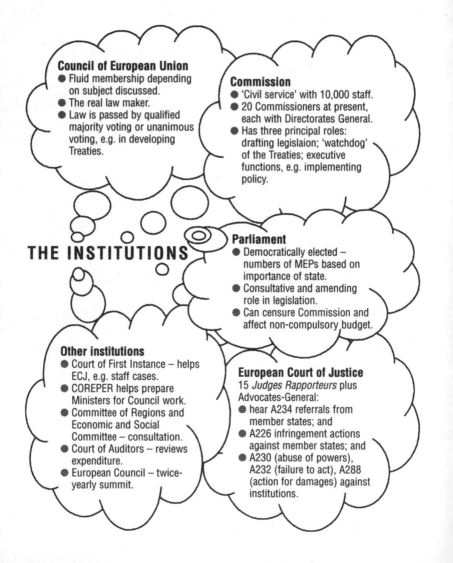

Council of European Union
- Fluid membership depending on subject discussed.
- The real law maker.
- Law is passed by qualified majority voting or unanimous voting, e.g. in developing Treaties.

Commission
- 'Civil service' with 10,000 staff.
- 20 Commissioners at present, each with Directorates General.
- Has three principal roles: drafting legislaion; 'watchdog' of the Treaties; executive functions, e.g. implementing policy.

THE INSTITUTIONS

Parliament
- Democratically elected – numbers of MEPs based on importance of state.
- Consultative and amending role in legislation.
- Can censure Commission and affect non-compulsory budget.

Other institutions
- Court of First Instance – helps ECJ, e.g. staff cases.
- COREPER helps prepare Ministers for Council work.
- Committee of Regions and Economic and Social Committee – consultation.
- Court of Auditors – reviews expenditure.
- European Council – twice-yearly summit.

European Court of Justice
15 *Judges Rapporteurs* plus Advocates-General:
- hear A234 referrals from member states; and
- A226 infringement actions against member states; and
- A230 (abuse of powers), A232 (failure to act), A288 (action for damages) against institutions.

2.1 THE DEVELOPMENT OF THE INSTITUTIONS

1. Concept and character of the institutions begins with the ECSC.
2. This required supranational bodies working independently of the member states.
3. The ECSC introduced the idea of 'community', with the following main features:
   - distinct legal personality;
   - represented by autonomous institutions;
   - member states ceded some national sovereignty to institutions for defined purposes.
4. The first institution was the 'High Authority', with power to make legally binding decisions.
   - Supplemented by a 'Common Assembly' – representative of member states.
   - Added to by a 'Special Council of Ministers' – with some legislative powers.
   - Completed initially by a 'Court of Justice' to 'ensure that the law was observed'.
5. EEC and EURATOM Treaties followed the same pattern.
   - Establishing 'communities' with four key institutions.
   - High Authority was replaced by a Commission with more limited powers.
6. A convention at the same time created a single Assembly and a single Court of Justice to represent all three communities.
7. The Brussels Treaty 1967 (Merger Treaty) established a single Council, and High Authority and two Commissions merged into one Commission – but communities kept separate identities.
8. The EC has a unique institutional structure:
   - it is not like any international organisation;
   - nor like a parliamentary democracy;
   - it has no clear separation of powers, but does have separation of interests;

- it has a complex legislative process and an executive without real executive powers;
- its institutions all have broad autonomy and their own rules of procedure;
- but the overriding ruler of the community is the Treaties – everything must conform with their objectives;
- and the Court of Justice exercises supervisory jurisdiction.

9. The Institutions have been added to over the years:
  - A4 EC Treaty led to an Economic and Social Committee and a Court of Auditors – made independent by TEU;
  - A4 also allowed COREPER – Committee of Permanent Representatives;
  - SEA established the Court of First Instance;
  - TEU created a Committee of the Regions;
  - TEU also provided for a European Investment Bank and European Central Bank.

10. The role of the institutions has also gradually changed:
  - new institutions have added complexity but not necessarily improvement;
  - the balance of power between Council and Commission has shifted;
  - Council's powers have increased;
  - Parliament's role has increased.

2.2 THE COUNCIL OF THE EUROPEAN UNION

1. This was formerly referred to as the Council of Ministers – since TEU it is the Council of the European Union.
2. The Council is a fluid concept with floating membership:
  - by A203 EC Treaty: 'Council shall consist of authorised representatives of each state';
  - the identity of the Minister depends on the subject of discussion;
  - but the original intention was a college of delegates.
3. The Council has a rotating presidency of six months. The

president is significant because he/she controls the agenda.

4. The Council is the major legislative organ, although there are some exceptions. It consults Parliament and Economic and Social Committees, but makes final decision on any legislation.

5. The voting procedure by A205 is of two main types:

- unanimous – required for certain proscribed areas and since Luxembourg Accords, if vital national interests at stake;
- qualified majority – with minimum of 62 votes carrying a measure, so designed to prevent big states abusing little ones, but originally designed to be used *per se*.

6. The qualified majority system is based on differential weighting according to the size and influence of the state:

- Germany, France, Italy, UK – 10 votes each
- Spain – 8 votes
- Belgium, Netherlands, Portugal, Greece – 5 votes each
- Sweden, Austria – 4 votes each
- Finland, Denmark, Ireland – 3 votes each
- Luxembourg – 2 votes

7. The Council has as its objective by A202, 'to ensure that the objectives set out in the Treaty are attained'.

8. But of course it is also a political body actually representing the interests of the individual member states.

9. The Council is supplemented by two further processes:

- European Council: twice-yearly meetings of heads of state and foreign ministers – a political summit;
- COREPER: a permanent committee representing member states – sifting through Commission proposals.

2.3 THE EUROPEAN COMMISSION

1. The Commission has the clearest claim to being a supranational body.

2. It is sometimes referred to as a civil service, but has much broader powers and roles.

3. It is currently comprised of 20 Commissioners:
- by A213 at least one from each state and not more than two – France, Germany, Italy UK, and Spain get two (Nice Treaty decided that from 2005 they will lose the extra commissioner, and with enlargement the number will be a maximum of 27, with a rotation system);
- chosen on grounds of general competence and 'whose independence is beyond doubt';
- they take an oath to be independent and not seek or take instructions from their member state (A213);
- their member state undertakes not to influence them;
- the appointment is for a five-year term;
- each Commissioner gets a Directorate General with specific responsibilities;
- the Commission also includes 10,000 staff.

4. The Commission is headed by a President, who holds office for a renewable two-year period.

5. The Commission is collegiate and acts by simple majority.

6. A211 sets out three principal responsibilities:
- It is initiator of legislation under A308 and can draft proposals on anything covered by the Treaties.
- It is watchdog of the Treaties – by A10 all member states are obliged to achieve the objectives of the Treaties, and the Commission can deal with breaches of EC law by member states through A226 proceedings.
- It has executive functions, for instance the Commission is responsible for implementing policy and also for the compulsory budget.

7. Through a process known as comity the Council can delegate power to the Commission, i.e. to produce detailed regulations following the passing of a framework regulation by the Council.

8. The Commission is sometimes also accountable to Parliament, e.g. Parliament can pass a motion of censure causing the Commission to resign.

2.4 THE EUROPEAN PARLIAMENT

1. This was originally known as the Assembly.
   - It was not democratically elected.
   - It comprised of appointed nominees from member state governments.
   - It had no legislative power and was only consultative.
2. It has been an elected body since 1979.
   - Elections are every five years.
   - Total membership is 626.
3. Membership depends on the size and importance of the particular member state:
   - the reunified Germany has .... 99 seats
   - France, Italy, UK have .... 87 seats each
   - Spain has .... 64 seats
   - Netherlands has .... 31 seats
   - Belgium, Greece, Portugal have ..... 25 seats each
   - Sweden has .... 22 seats
   - Austria has .... 21 seats
   - Denmark, Finland have .... 16 seats each
   - Ireland has .... 15 seats
   - Luxembourg has .... 6 seats
4. By Treaty of Amsterdam (ToA) an upper limit of 700 seats has been set in the case of an enlarged EU.
5. MEPs sit by political groupings rather than by national interest, and there is no mandatory voting for member state interests – MEPs are representatives not delegates.
6. Voting is on a majority basis, with 314 votes needed to pass any measure.
7. Parliament elects its own President and officials
8. Parliament enjoys three main powers at present:
   - it can censure the Commission (and such a censure in 1999 led to the resignation of the entire Commission);
   - it has powers over the non-compulsory budget;
   - it has a consultative role in legislation:
     (i) consultation procedure;

(ii) co-operation procedure (under SEA);

(iii) co-decision procedure (under TEU); and

(iv) assent.

2.5 THE EUROPEAN COURT OF JUSTICE

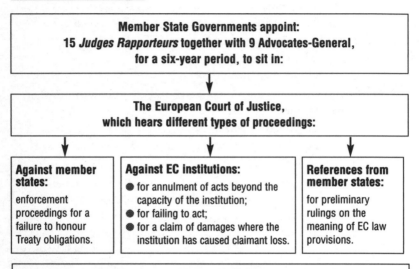

Member State Governments appoint:
15 *Judges Rapporteurs* together with 9 Advocates-General,
for a six-year period, to sit in:

The European Court of Justice,
which hears different types of proceedings:

Against member states:
enforcement proceedings for a failure to honour Treaty obligations.

Against EC institutions:
● for annulment of acts beyond the capacity of the institution;
● for failing to act;
● for a claim of damages where the institution has caused claimant loss.

References from member states:
for preliminary rulings on the meaning of EC law provisions.

Court of First Instance (12 Judges) hears different actions:
● direct actions by natural and legal persons (not anti-dumping);
● staff cases;
● some cases under ECSC.

The work of the ECJ and CFI

1. This is not like any court in the English legal system.

2. It is composed of 15 *Judges Rapporteurs* (the judges) and these are assisted by nine Advocates General:
- one judge is appointed from each state;
- by A233 they must be independent beyond doubt and judges or legal academics in their own country;
- they each serve a six-year term;
- but there is a staggered re-appointment system;

- removal of a judge is only possible if all colleagues agree that (s)he is unfit to serve;
- they appoint a president from their number;
- majority decision rules, with inquisitorial procedure and no dissenting judgments;
- most issues involving member states or an institution are heard by a full court, but some straightforward issues can be heard by a bench of three or five;
- Advocates General are appointed with the same requirements as for judges;
- Cases are assigned to one of these first, who produces a reasoned opinion for the court – this does not have to be followed by the court but it may be.

3. The role of the court according to A220 is:
- to ensure that in application and interpretation the law is observed;
- and to provide a forum for resolving disputes between institutions, member states, and individuals;
- and to protect individual rights.

4. The court hears five main types of action:
- A234 references from member states for a preliminary ruling on an interpretation of EC law (known also as indirect actions);
- A226 actions against Member States for failing to implement Treaty obligations (a direct action known also as infringement proceedings);
- A230 actions against an institution for abuse of power;
- A232 actions against an institution for a failure to act;
- A288 actions for damages against an institution that has been responsible for loss to the individual, e.g. where the Commission has failed to address a decision to a body engaging in anti-competitive practices and an individual suffers loss as a result.

5. It is important to note that the ECJ has been responsible for defining the Treaties and in particular has been instrumental in ensuring their enforcement through many landmark

decisions, e.g. defining and developing the principles of supremacy, direct effect, indirect effect, state liability, etc.

6. Because of the excess workload of the ECJ and resultant delays, SEA also created a Court of First Instance (CFI):
   - It has similar requirements to the ECJ.
   - Its basic purpose is to ease the workload of the ECJ (but has had limited success in doing so).
   - It only takes on limited specific cases, e.g. staff cases.
   - A234 references are specifically excluded.
   - There is a possible right of appeal to the ECJ.

2.6 THE OTHER MAJOR INSTITUTIONS

1. Besides the four main institutions of Council, Commission, Parliament and European Court of Justice, there are a number of other important institutions – the first three have already been referred to

2. The European Council:
   - a twice-yearly summit of the heads of state and foreign ministers, focusing on political matters;
   - in 1999 it gave a brief to the intergovernmental conference (IGC) to keep under review: the size and composition of the EC; weighting of votes in the Council of Ministers; extension to qualified majority voting.

3. COREPER – the Committee of Permanent Representatives:
   - It is a permanent body of representatives from member states, because of the fluid membership of the Council.
   - It examines the Commission's legislative proposals for individual ministers.

4. The Court of First Instance:
   - set up initially in the Single European Act (SEA);
   - usually sits with three or five judges;
   - jurisdiction is limited to staff cases, competition cases, anti-dumping cases;
   - since 1993 it can hear all cases brought by natural or legal persons (including judicial review), but not those brought

by the institutions or by the member states.

5. The Court of Auditors:
- This was created in 1975.
- It was designed to control and supervise the community budget.
- It was made a full institution by TEU.
- It has 15 qualified members.
- It examines accounts of all revenue and expenditure.

6. The Economic and Social Committee (ESC):
- Membership is based on representation of social and economic activities, e.g. farmers, carriers, dealers, craftsmen, etc.
- It has a consultative role within both the EC and EURATOM, with ECSC having a similar process.
- It is consulted by either the Council or the Commission wherever they deem that it is appropriate to consult.
- It has 189 members who are appointed by the Council.

7. The Committee of the Regions:
- This came into being in 1994 after TEU, under A263–265.
- It has membership comes from local and regional bodies, but not local or national government.
- It has 222 members.
- It has a consultative role and is designed to bring regional influence to EC legislation.
- It usually gives opinions on things like education and training, culture, health, environmental issues and social cohesion.

8. The European Central Bank (ECB):
- In TEU provision was made in the Protocol to have a Central Bank to act for the EU.
- It is obviously a vital element of economic monetary union and the single currency.
- From January 1999 it has had responsibility for monetary policy in the EU.
- It is the only body allowed to issues euro banknotes.

CHAPTER 3

THE SOURCES OF EUROPEAN LAW

Primary Sources	The Treaties: ECSC; EURATOM; EC; SEA; TEU; ToA; ToN. Divides into: ● Procedural Treaty Articles, e.g. A249 which identifies the legislation; or A226 an action against a member state. ● Substantive Treaty Articles, e.g. A141 Equal pay for men and women; or A39 the free movement of workers.	
Secondary Sources	**Legislation:**	
	Regulations	Automatically law in member states. They are generally applicable, binding in their entirety, and directly applicable.
	Directives	Binding as to the effect to be achieved. Member states have an implementing period within which they must be incorporated in national law by whatever method.
	Decisions	Addressed to a specific party, whether a company, individual, or member state. They are then binding in their entirety on the party to whom they are addressed.
	Recommendations	Have no legal force but are persuasive.
	Opinions	Have no legal force but are persuasive.
Tertiary Sources	**Case law of European Court of Justice** Vital because of: ● the power to ensure observance of treaty objectives through A234 references; ● the judicial creativity of the ECJ in comparison to the relative inertia of the legislative bodies. **General Principles:** ● proportionality, equality, legal certainty; ● protection of fundamental human rights; ● subsidiarity. Acts adopted by representatives of Member State Governments meeting in Council. National law of Member States. Public International law.	

The sources of EC law

3.1 PRIMARY SOURCES – THE TREATIES

3.1.1 The structure of the EC Treaty

1. This begins with a preamble, which is useful for the ECJ for interpretation purposes.
2. It is then split into six parts:
   - principles – ground rules;
   - citizenship – added by TEU and now in A17;
   - policies of the Community – effectively the legal order;
   - references to overseas relationships;
   - the institutions – empowerment and identification of roles, etc.;
   - general and final provisions, e.g. to enter into other treaties.
3. It also includes annexes, protocols, and declarations.
4. The substantive law of the Treaty is also contained in numerous Articles.

3.1.2 The principles

1. These are the 'tasks' of the Community:
   - A2 identifies in general terms the 'economic, social and political' tasks.
   - The most immediate of these is the creation of a 'common market' – 'the elimination of all obstacles to intra-Community trade in order to merge the national markets into a single market ...'.
   - This has since been supplemented by the addition of an 'economic and monetary union'.
2. A3 sets out the principal activities:
   - elimination of customs duties, quantitative restrictions and other measures having equivalent effect;
   - common commercial policy;
   - an internal market;

- measures concerning the entry and movement of people within an internal market;
- common agriculture and fisheries policies;
- common transport policies;
- measures ensuring the prevention of anti-competitive practices;
- harmonisation of national law to allow a common market to function.

3. A3 seeks to ensure that the Community acts within the limits of its powers and for the objectives assigned to it.
4. A10 identifies the obligations of the member states:
   - 'to take all appropriate measures ... to ensure fulfillment of the objectives arising out of the Treaty ...'
   - 'to abstain from any measure which could jeopardise the attainment of the objectives ...'
5. A12 identifies basic principle of non-discrimination on the basis of nationality.

3.1.3 The Community policies

1. These are found in Part 3.
2. The most important are the 'Four Freedoms':
   - free movement of goods (agriculture as a special category);
   - free movement of persons;
   - free movement of services (transport as a special category);
   - free movement of capital.
3. Free movement of goods provides for the elimination of customs duties and quantitative restrictions between member states to products originating in member states, and products coming from non-member states that are 'in free circulation':
   - A25 governs the customs union – elimination of duties, etc.;
   - A28 and A29 cover non-tariff barriers – elimination of quotas.
4. Agriculture is subject to complex rules and a Common Agricultural Policy (CAP).

5. Free movement of persons and services are both guaranteed under the Treaties in A39, A43 and A49, and workers' families are also given protections in secondary legislation.
6. A common transport policy is also envisaged in the Treaty.
7. Free movement of capital is contained in TEU, all restrictions on movement of capital and payments is prohibited, and now policy is ultimately driven towards economic and monetary union.
8. Other main EC policies include:
   * rules on anti-competitive practices in A81 and A82;
   * tax provisions in A90;
   * anti-discrimination in A141.

3.1.4 Rules on the institutions and on procedure

1. One of the most important procedural Articles is A249, which identifies and explains the different forms of legislation.
2. The relationship with member states is partly defined in A234, which provides the mechanism for gaining interpretations of EC law from the ECJ.
3. The general rules regarding each of the institutions are in the EC Treaty:
   * Parliament in A189–A199;
   * Council in A202–A207;
   * Commission in A211–A214;
   * ECJ in A220–A245.

3.1.5 The general and final provisions

1. Provides Community has a legal personality – so under A310 it can make arrangements with other international bodies.
2. The Community can be liable through its institutions (A288).
3. Powers are also given to member states to derogate from Treaty obligations in certain extreme circumstances, e.g. security, serious internal disturbance or threat of external conflict, balance of payments crises.

4. The Council has very broad powers under A308 to legislate to do anything that is 'necessary to attain ... an objective of the Community ...'.

3.2 SECONDARY SOURCES – REGULATIONS, DIRECTIVES AND DECISIONS

3.2.1 The acts of the institutions

1. Secondary legislation is a collective term used to describe all the various types of law the institutions can make.
2. They are subordinate to primary law (the Treaties), and so cannot amend, repeal or alter the scope of a primary instrument.
3. So the Institutions may only act:
   - in order to carry out their tasks;
   - in strict accordance with the provisions of the Treaties;
   - within the limits of the powers conferred upon them in the Treaties, specifically A249.
4. The EC Treaty at A249 provides that: 'In order to carry out their tasks and in accordance with the provisions of this Treaty, the European Parliament acting jointly with the Council [added by TEU], the Council and the Commission shall make regulations and issue directives, take decisions, make recommendations or deliver opinions.'
5. The various forms of secondary legislation are described in A249 and it is their scope and effect that distinguishes them from each other.

3.2.2 Regulations

1. By A249: 'A regulation shall have general application. It shall be binding in its entirety and directly applicable in all Member States.'
   - 'General application' means it applies to all member states.
   - 'Binding in its entirety' means member states have no choice but to give effect to the regulation in its entirety.

- 'Directly applicable' means the regulation automatically becomes law in each member state with no requirement for the state to do anything to implement it, and it may create rights and obligations directly enforceable in the national courts (*Bussone v Ministry of Agriculture* (1978)).

2. Regulations enter into force on the date specified in them.

3.2.3 Directives

1. By A249: 'A directive shall be binding, as to the result to be achieved, upon each member state to which it is addressed, but shall leave to the national authorities the choice of form and methods.'

2. Directives are unlike regulations (which are uniform and directly applicable rules):
- they are used to ensure that member states adapt their own laws for the application of common standards;
- they require member states to choose the method of implementation within a set deadline;
- they are mainly used in areas where the diversity of national laws could have a harmful effect on the establishment or functioning of the common market.

3. So, whereas a regulation is applicable to member states and individual citizens alike, a directive:
- is primarily intended to create legal obligations on the member state;
- so is not intended to create directly enforceable rights for individuals, but the ECJ ensures that it does.

4. However, there are now important exceptions to this last point:
- vertical direct effect, which may be relied upon by the individual in the case of unimplemented directives if the claim is against the state or an 'emanation of the state' (*van Duyn* and *Ratti* and, of course, *Marshall* and, for an indication of what amounts to an emanation of the state, see also UK cases such as *Foster v British Gas* and *Doughty v Rolls-Royce*);
- the duty of 'uniform interpretation', which the ECJ

derives from A10 EC Treaty. Where there is a divergence between national law and the directive, the national law must be interpreted so as to give effect to the directive even where it remains unimplemented (the *Von Colson* principle, as developed by *Marleasing*) – the so-called principle of 'indirect effect');

● the *Francovich* principle, that while there can be no horizontal direct effect based on a directive as between non-state parties, an individual who has suffered loss as a result of the member state's failure to implement a directive may claim damages from the state (so-called 'state liability' – *Grad v Finanzamt Traustein 9/70*).

3.2.4 Decisions

1. By A249: 'A decision shall be binding in its entirety upon those to whom it is addressed.'

2. The first feature of a decision is that it is the least easy to define of the legislative acts – it could be a legally binding measure in a specific legal form, but it could also be a non-binding, informal act laying down guidelines.

3. Its most striking effect is that it is immediately and totally binding on the addressee, and as a result may create rights for third parties.

	General applicability	Direct applicability	Direct effect
Treaty articles	Yes – they apply throughout the community	Once Treaty is incorporated there is no need for further enactment of Articles	Yes – if they conform to the *Van Gend* criteria
Regulations	Yes – they apply throughout the community	Yes – they require no further implementation	Yes – if they conform to the *Van Gend* criteria
Directives	Yes – they will be addressed to all states	No – they are an order, so require implementation	Only vertically if unimplemented or incorrectly implemented
Decisions	No – they are addressed to a particular individual	They are an order that must be complied with by the addressee	They may confer rights on other individuals affected by them

The effects of primary and secondary law

3.3 THE PROCESS OF LEGISLATING

3.3.1 Introduction

1. The process of legislating has been modified significantly as the result of different Treaties – one of the most significant features of the early legislative process was the so-called 'democratic deficit'.
2. There are basically four types of legislative procedure that are now possible within the community legal order:
   - the proposal (or consultation) procedure;
   - the co-operation procedure;
   - the co-decision procedure;
   - assent.
3. The proposal procedure was the original legislative procedure in existence before the SEA.
4. Following SEA the co-operation procedure was introduced to provide a straightforward method, involving the European Parliament (two readings) and to be passed by qualified majority voting for internal market measures – in fact this has been largely removed by the Treaty of Amsterdam, and only survives in respect of EMU.
5. TEU introduced the co-decision procedure, which has subsequently been modified or simplified by ToA.
6. The assent procedure, which is similar to the co-decision procedure, was introduced first in SEA and extended by TEU.

3.3.2 The proposal procedure

1. This is still the basis for the adoption of all general EC instruments.
2. So it is applicable where none of the other procedures apply.
3. It basically rests on the idea that the Commission 'proposes' and the Council 'disposes'.
4. However, it also depends on consultation with Parliament and the Economic and Social Committee or the Committee of the Regions, and discussions in COREPER.

5. Failure to genuinely consult is a breach of an essential procedural requirement, so may result in a measure being declared void (*SA Roquette Freres v Council 138/7*).

EC SECONDARY LEGISLATION

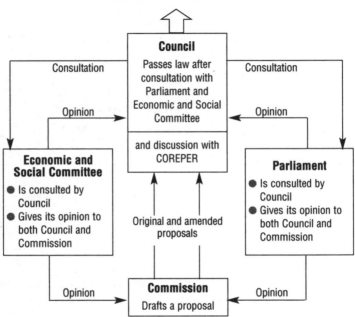

The proposal procedure of legislating

3.3.3 The co-operation procedure

1. This was introduced by SEA to give a greater role to Parliament in the legislative process.
2. It was also designed to be a simple means for the adoption of measures affecting the internal market.
3. The process involved qualified majority voting by Council.
4. It was actually inspired by the proposal procedure, but was designed to be a much quicker procedure.
5. The 'democratic deficit' was supposedly reduced by the inclusion of two 'readings' of the measure before Parliament.

6. With the exception of issues concerning Economic and Monetary Union, it has now been replaced by the co-decision procedure.

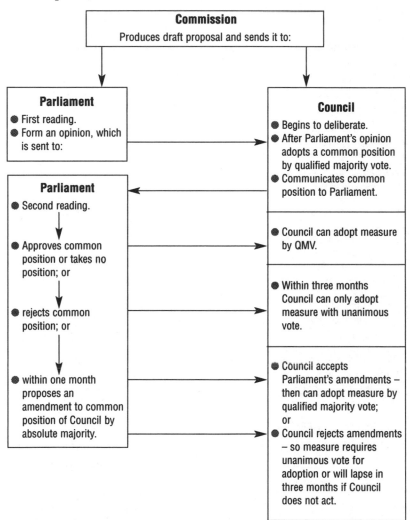

The stages in the co-operation procedure

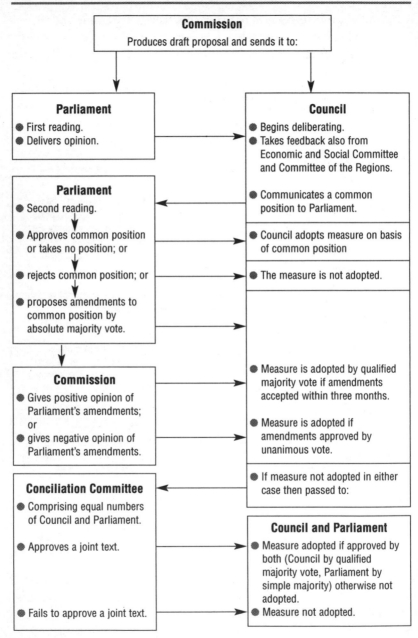

The co-decision procedure

3.3.4 The co-decision procedure

1. This was introduced by TEU and simplified by the Treaty of Amsterdam.
2. It gives more power to Parliament, i.e. after Parliament proposing amendments, the Council must consider them and if they reject them then the act is not adopted, but final adoption of measure is still with the Council.
3. There is also the possibility of a 'Conciliation Committee' made up of equal representation from Council and Parliament if Council does not accept all amendments.
4. It has replaced the co-operation procedure in relation to internal market measures, and applies also to, for example, environment, transport, consumer protection, culture.

3.3.5 Assent

1. This is just a modified version of the co-decision procedure.
2. It was introduced in SEA and extended in TEU.
3. Measures can only be adopted if having the positive approval of both Council and Parliament.
4. It is used in respect to measures on international agreements under A310, rights of EU citizens under A18, elections to Parliament under A107, and also human rights issues after the Treaty of Amsterdam, and enlargement of the EU.

3.4 NON-BINDING SECONDARY LEGISLATION

1. A249 introduces the concept of 'soft laws', referring specifically to recommendations and opinions, but adds: 'Recommendations and opinions have no binding force.'
2. While having no legal force, they can be issued on any matter dealt with in the Treaties, but may be persuasive, particularly politically and morally.
3. Since TEU increasing use has been made of soft laws, particularly within the social context.

4. A classic example is the EC Commission Code of Practice on Sexual Harassment:
   - while the Code is not binding it should not be ignored;
   - indeed it provides the UK definition of sexual harassment which otherwise would not exist, and has been applied (*Insitu Cleaning Co. v Heads* (1995)).

3.5 GENERAL PRINCIPLES OF LAW

3.5.1 General

1. These are often unwritten principles (but not always, e.g. equality – A141, etc.).
2. These are generally developed by the ECJ, using as its authority A220 EC – the general duty on the Court of Justice to ensure that community law is observed.
3. They are nevertheless binding on the institutions, the member states and individual citizens.
4. General principles are a familiar concept to those states with a 'civil' Roman law tradition.
5. So they are in essentially a statement of values and basic standards that the court will use in interpretation.
6. They are broad enough to be generally acceptable as principle, but specific application can cause controversy.
7. Since much EC law is essentially administrative, some principles have derived from administrative law of France and Germany, but some has also derived from UK law.

3.5.2 Proportionality

1. This is now written into the EC Treaty at A3b paragraph 3 by TEU: 'Any action by the Community shall not go beyond what is necessary to achieve the objectives of this treaty.'
2. The means used must be proportionate to the end to be achieved.
3. It derives from a German principle, *verhalthismassigkeit.*

4. First stated in the *International Handelgesselschaft Case 5/73*: 'No burdens should be placed on the citizens except to the extent that it is necessary to achieve the purpose.'
5. So, if the burden is too great the court can disapply the measure (see *Bela Muhler Bergman v Grows Farm 114/76* and *Watson (Lynne) and Alessandro Belmann 118/75*).

3.5.3 Equality

1. A general principle of equal treatment and non-discrimination.
2. Equal situations must always be treated equally unless there are objective justifications for doing otherwise.
3. Specific provision under A12: no discrimination on nationality.
4. The treaty also contains specific provisions eliminating discrimination between men and women e.g. A141.
5. But the principle also obviously applies in internal organisation (*Sabbatini v Parliament 20/71*).
6. A similar line has been extended to questions of religion (*Prais v The Council 130/75*).
7. There are also new directives specifically on discrimination.

3.5.4 Legal certainty and procedural rights

1. The basic principle is that the law in its application must be predictable. So:
   * there should be no retroactive laws (*Société pour l'exploitation des sucres v Commission 88/76*);
   * there will be respect for acquired rights, which cannot later be withdrawn;
   * a person is entitled to act according to legitimate expectations, i.e. as though the law still applies (*Commission v Council 81/72*);
   * persons affected should be identifiable;
   * language should be easily understood;

- a person is entitled to a fair hearing (*Transocean Marine Paint Association v The Commission 17/74*). Also found in some secondary legislation, e.g. directive 64/221 derogations on free movement.

3.5.5 The protection of fundamental human rights

1. Now contained in A6(1): 'shall respect fundamental rights guaranteed by the European Convention ... and from the constitutional traditions common to the member states...'.

2. A number of propositions emerge from this:
- *audi alteram partem* – fair hearings before imposition of a penalty (*Transocean Marine Paint*);
- penalty must be based on a clear, unambiguous case;
- no retroactive laws;
- no one should be subjected to two penalties;
- entitlement to legal assistance and representation;
- a person is protected from self-incrimination, so no requirement to answer leading questions;
- respect for private life and inviolability of premises (*X v Commission 404/92*).

3. It originates from the constitutions of certain member states (*The International Handelgesselschaft Case 11/70*).

4. But the ECJ is prepared to recognise the significance of human rights (*Nold v The Commission 4/73*).

5. Although the EU is not a signatory to the European Convention of Human Rights it is possible to invoke Articles of the Convention (*R v Kirk 63/83*).

6. There is now also a Charter of Rights accepted at the Nice Summit.

3.5.6 Subsidiarity

1. There is some reference to subsidiarity in the founding Treaties – decisions should be taken as closely as possible to citizens affected by them.

2. It was incorporated in the EC Treaty as A5 by TEU at the UK's insistence: 'In areas which do not fall within its exclusive competence, the community shall take action, in accordance with the principle of subsidiarity, only if and in so far as the objectives of the proposed action cannot be sufficiently achieved by the member states and can therefore, by reason of the scale or effects of the proposed action, be better achieved by the community.'

3. So there is a two-fold test – Community action can only be justified if it serves an end which:
   - cannot be achieved satisfactorily at national level; and
   - can be achieved better at community level.

3.6 CASE LAW OF THE ECJ

1. Unlike English law, continental 'civil' systems have no binding system of precedent, and the ECJ follows the same principles.

2. Any binding force in the judgement then rests on the principle of *res judicita*.

3. So, for future cases ECJ judgements act as moral rather than strictly legal authority, and in the strictest technical sense then the court's judgements are not a formal source of law.

4. However, there are a number of qualifying points:
   - the court will not depart from its own rulings on law without pressing reasons, and judgements, if studied, show remarkable consistency;
   - a ruling in a particular case has an inevitable impact beyond the case itself;
   - the *Cilfit* rules on A234 references prevent repetitious references seeking new rulings on the same principle of law;
   - the ECJ has proved over the years to be very proactive;
   - indeed, many of the most definitive principles of EC law have originated in the ECJ, e.g. direct effect, indirect effect, state liability, etc.

CHAPTER 4

ENFORCEMENT OF EC LAW

A226 infringement proceedings against member states
- Usually brought by Commission as watchdog.
- Three clear purposes:
  - (i) to ensure member states comply with Treaties;
  - (ii) to provide a procedure for dispute resolution;
  - (iii) to provide means of clarifying law.
- Starts with mediation, then three formal stages:
  - (i) notice of default;
  - (ii) reasoned opinion;
  - (iii) proceedings in ECJ.
- Penalites possible in A228.
- An action by another state possible under A227 (*France v UK*).

ENFORCEMENT (DIRECT ACTIONS)

A230 Actions agains institutions for abus of power:
- Two major functions:
  - (i) provides way of controlling legality of binding acts;
  - (ii) gives legal protection to those subject to Community instruments adversely affected by illegal ones.
- Commission, Council, member states are privileged claimants.
- Natural and legal persons gain *locus standi* for a decision addressed to them or a regulation or a decision addressed to another person of direct and individual concern to them.
- Individual concern means decision affects them because of attributes (*Plaumann v Commission*).
- A Regulacion may be challenged if it has no general application but is a 'bundle of individual Decisions' (*International Fruit Co. v Commission*).
- Grounds for review include: lack of competence, infringement of an essential procedural requirement, infringement of Treaties or procedural rules, misuse of powers.

A232 Actions against institutions for failing to act:
- Can challenge commission, Council, Parliament, European Central Bank.
- Privileged claimants are member states and institutions.
- Natural and legal persons must show institution failed to address to them any instrument other than an opinion or recommendation.
- Grounds for review are where applicant can show he was entitled to a Decision and none was addressed to him, or an action has not been taken which is of direct and individual concern to him.

A288 actions for damages against institutions:
- 'To make good any damage caused by institutions.'
- Almost unrestricted *locus standi*.
- D must be an institution or its servant, not Community as a whole (*Werhahn Hansamuhle v Council*).
- Conditions for liability are:
  - (i) damage suffered by claimant;
  - (ii) fault of institution;
  - (iii) causal connection.

4.1 ENFORCEMENT: INTRODUCTION

1. Substantive rights and obligations granted under Treaties would be ineffective if left merely to the co-operation of member states.
2. Individual rights may be abused by EC institutions and by member states.
3. So, a variety of enforcement proceedings and methods for reviewing the actions of both institutions and member states were created in the Treaty, placed under the scrutiny of the ECJ, with individuals able to gain remedies.
4. These procedures are known as 'direct actions' and supplement 'indirect actions' of A234 reference procedure.
5. The measures are broad in that they allow a wide range of applicants to initiate proceedings.

4.2 A226 INFRINGEMENT PROCEEDINGS AGAINST MEMBER STATES

4.2.1 Introduction

1. EC law depends on a partnership with member states, e.g. in the implementation of directives.
2. But it is not uncommon for member states to be careless or even reluctant in fulfilling their obligations.
3. So, the Treaty provides the means of calling member states to account.
4. It is normally invoked by the Commission under A226.
5. But it can be initiated by other member states under A227.

4.2.2 Actions by the Commission under A226

1. Commission is 'watchdog of Treaties' so is empowered by A226 to monitor behaviour of member states and enforce compliance with Treaty obligations if necessary.

2. By A226: 'if Commission considers a member state has failed to fulfil an obligation ... it shall deliver a reasoned opinion on the matter after giving state concerned opportunity to submit its observations. If state concerned does not comply ... within period laid down [Commission] may bring matter before Court of Justice.'

3. So A226 has three clear purposes:
   - to ensure member states comply with Treaty obligations;
   - to provide a procedure for dispute resolution;
   - to provide means of clarifying law for all member states.

4. There are three formal stages in the procedure – but these are usually preceded by an informal stage.
   - Mediation (informal): the Commission engages in discussions with the member state, which will usually remedy the error at this point. The action is then discontinued.
   - Formal notice of default:
     (i) where the Commission remains dissatisfied it issues a notice inviting the member state to submit its own observations;
     (ii) this stage defines the terms of reference which are then fixed (*Commission v Italy (Re Payment of Export Rebates) 31/69*).
   - Reasoned opinion:
     (i) issued if the member state still fails to comply;
     (ii) sets out reasons why the member state is in default and a time limit;
     (iii) but is not itself binding (*Alfonse Lutticke GmbH v Hauptzollamt Saarlouis 57/65*).
   - Court proceedings in the ECJ:
     (i) the Commission brings an action if the member state still fails to comply;
     (ii) but the issue can still be settled without a court decision, e.g. interim relief under A243;
     (iii) many defences have been tried, but most fail:
        a) internal difficulties (*Commission v Belgium 77/69*).

    b) reciprocity (*Commission v France (Re restrictions on lamb imports) 232/78*);

    c) *force majeure* (*Commission v Italy 101/84*);

    d) objections by trade unions (*Commission v UK 128/78*).

5. Enforcement:

- before TEU the ECJ's decisions were incapable of actual enforcement, so more A226 proceedings were used;
- now, by A228, a financial penalty is possible, e.g. *Commission v Greece C-387/97*.

4.2.3 Actions brought by member states under A227

1. This was always intended to be an exceptional procedure.

2. However, it is a useful safeguard against errors of judgement by the Commission.

3. It is a similar procedure, though the member state should work closely with the Commission in preliminary stages.

4. Only one case has been brought so far – *France v UK 141/78*.

4.3 A230 ACTIONS AGAINST INSTITUTIONS FOR EXCEEDING POWERS

4.3.1 Introduction

1. A230 is one of the few instances by which individuals can bring action in the ECJ, though their ability to do so is more restricted than for institutions.

2. The procedure has two major functions:

- it provides a means of controlling the legality of binding acts of Community institutions;
- it gives legal protection to those subject to Community instruments adversely affected by illegal ones.

4.3.2 Locus standi

1. Member states, the Commission and the Council are all named in A230.
   - So are all 'privileged claimants' with virtually unlimited rights of challenge (except for recommendations and opinions).
   - Provided the measure complained of has binding effect on the claimant.
2. Parliament and the European Central Bank are privileged claimants but with more limited powers of challenge. They may only bring an action 'for the purpose of protecting their prerogatives'.
3. Natural and legal persons also gain *locus standi* by A230, but rights of challenge are limited to 'a Decision addressed to that person, or a decision which, although in the form of a Regulation or a Decision addressed to another person, is of direct and individual concern to the individual...'.
4. So, except in the case of decisions addressed to the individual, there are three key issues to be established:
   - What is individual concern?
     (i) The decision must affect the applicant 'by reason of certain attributes which are peculiar to them or by reason of circumstances in which they are differentiated from all other persons and by virtue of these factors distinguishes them individually just as ... person addressed ...' (*Plaumann v Commission 25/62*).
     (ii) Since modified to extent it must be possible to determine the identity of persons affected at the time the measure complained of was adopted (*Toepfler v Commission 106 and107/63*).
     (iii) The ECJ has said there must be a 'closed group' of people affected (*International Fruit Co. v Commission 41-44/70*).
     (iv) However, there is inconsistent application (*Piraiki-Patraiki v Commission 11/82*).

- What is direct concern?
  - (i) It is different from individual concern, but still subject to inconsistent interpretation.
  - (ii) As well as causal connection it refers to 'immediate, automatic and inevitable disadvantageous legal effects' without need for further intervention (*Alcan Aluminium Raeren et al v Commission 69/69*).
  - (iii) However, this strict standard has since been relaxed (*Bock v Commission 62/70 (The Chinese Mushrooms Case)*).
- When is a Regulation to be seen as a Decision affecting the applicant?
  - (i) Genuine Regulations are never capable of challenge by an individual (*Calpak SpA v Commission 789/79*).
  - (ii) So, a Regulation must fit the label given to it – *Confederation Nationale des Producteurs de Fruits et Legumes v Council 16 and 17/72*: 'what distinguishes a Regulation is not the greater or lesser extent of its application, material or territorial, but the fact that its provisions apply impersonally in objective situations ...'.
  - (iii) So, a Regulation may be challenged when it has no general application but is 'a bundle of individual Decisions taken by the Commission, each of which, although taken in the form of a Regulation, affected the legal position of the applicant ...' (*International Fruit Co. v Commission 41-44/70*).

4.3.3 Substantive grounds for review

1. Once admissibility is established the claimant must show that the challenge concerns one of four grounds identified in Article.
2. Lack of competence:
   - there is no direct comparison in English law, but seen as comparable to the *ultra vires* doctrine;

- it occurs if an institution exercises a power not conferred upon it by EC law, or exercises a non-existent power, or encroaches on the power of another institution;
- the ECJ has defined the ground but will rarely accept challenges between institutions (*Commission v Council (Re European Road Transport Agreement) 22/70 (The ERTA case)*);
- so, it is more likely to be used for powers not possessed at all (*Ford (Europe) v Commission 228 and 229/82*);
- or often for improper delegation (*Meroni v High Authority 9/56*).

3. Infringement of an essential procedural requirement:
- EC law imposes procedural requirements as safeguards.
- Essential procedures include:
  (i) preparation e.g. prior consultation *Roquette Freres v Council 138/79*;
  (ii) communication giving reasons *Germany v Commission 52 and 55/65*.

4. Infringement of Treaties or rules relating to their application:
- allows the ECJ to review whether the acts of the institutions conform to EC law;
- can include all aspects, e.g. general principles, so any sort of violation of EC law will be invalid (*Transocean Marine Paint Association v Commission 17/74*).

5. Misuse of powers:
- refers to institution using a power it possesses but for objects contrary to those for which it was granted;
- may include any illegitimate use of power (*Bock v Commission 62/70 (The Chinese Mushrooms case)*).

4.3.4 Procedure

1. The most important requirement is a strict time limit for bringing an action.
2. This is two months from date on which the measure was published, was notified to the claimant or came to his attention – but this may be extended if there are unforeseeable circumstances or *force majeure*.

3. The consequences of a successful claim is for the instrument to be declared void by the ECJ.

4.4 A232 ACTIONS AGAINST INSTITUTIONS FOR A FAILURE TO ACT

4.4.1 General

1. A232 allows member states and Community institutions to challenge the Council, Commission, Parliament, and European Central Bank for not acting when they should.
2. It is the natural corollary of A230 proceedings.
3. Applicants must satisfy admissibility and show suitable grounds for review.

4.4.2 Admissibility

1. Three conditions must be met.
2. Title to sue (*locus standi*):
   - 'privileged claimants' are 'member states and other institutions', which now includes Parliament (*Parliament v Council 377/87*);
   - 'natural and legal persons' can bring action against a Community institution which failed to address to that person any instrument other than a recommendation or an opinion.
3. It must be an indictable institution – the Council, Commission, Parliament or the Central Bank.
4. A prior approach to the institution:
   - must be made by the applicant before applying to the ECJ;
   - it must be explicit and refer to the possibility of A232 if no reply within two months.

4.4.3 Grounds for Review

1. Will be where the applicant can show he was entitled to a decision and none was addressed to him, or an action has not been taken which is of direct and individual concern to him.
2. Few cases are admissible so there are few guidelines.
3. Generally, if there is a result to be achieved and an obligation is sufficiently well defined then any attempt to disregard it will fall within scope of A232 (*Parliament v Council 13/83*).

4.5 A288 ACTIONS FOR DAMAGES

4.5.1 General

1. A288(2) states: 'In the case of non-contractual liability, the Community shall ... make good any damage caused by the Institutions or by its servants in the performance of their duties'.
2. So, it is a general tort action but based more on French civil law.

4.5.2 Admissibility

1. *Locus standi* is almost unrestricted – any natural or legal person can claim provided the party him/herself has suffered damage resulting from an act or omission of an institution or its servant.
2. The defendant must be an institution or its servant, not the Community as a whole (*Werhahn Hansamuhle v Council 63-69/72*).
3. The appropriate time limit is five years from the date of the event giving rise to the action.

4.5.3 Conditions for liability

1. Three elements must be satisfied for a successful claim.
2. Damage suffered by the claimant:

- can be any damage that is certain, provable and quantifiable;
- future loss is recoverable in some circumstances (*Kampffmeyer et al v Commission 5,7 and 13-24/66*);
- even highly speculative loss is recoverable in some circumstances (*Adams v Commission 145/83*).

3. Fault on the part of the institution complained of:
   - it is only necessary to show that the claimant was owed a duty which was breached (*Adams v Commission 145/83*);
   - but the ECJ is less likely to conclude fault where the institution makes policy decisions and errs (*Zuckerfabrik Schoppenstedt v Council 5/71*).

4. A causal connection between measure and damage:
   - proof of damage alone is insufficient for liability without proof that the act of the institution directly caused it (*Dumortier Freres SA v Council 27,28 and 45/79*);
   - so remoteness is an important factor (*Pool v Council 49/79*).

CHAPTER 5

THE RELATIONSHIP BETWEEN EC LAW AND NATIONAL LAW

EC LAW AND NATIONAL LAW

Supremacy:
- Vital to ensure supranational character of institutions, but not mentioned in Treaties.
- First stated in *Van Gend en Loos* – states have given up sovereignty to new legal order.
- Explained in *Costa v ENEL*– clear limitation of sovereign right upon which subsequent unilateral law, incompatible with aims of Community, cannot prevail.
- Any conflict is settled in favour of EC law (*Simmenthal*).
- Following *R v Secretary of State for Transport ex parte Factortame No (2)* national court can do everything necessary to set aside national legislative provisions which might prevent Community rules from having full force and effect.

A234 References:
- Means of ensuring uniform applications of EC law.
- Any court may refer – some have mandatory referral.
- ECJ test in *CILFIT* of where reference unnecessary: where EC law irrelevant or peripheral; or where there is an existing interpretation; or where correct interpretation is so obvious that no doubt.
- *Fogilla v Novella*: reference must involve genuine issue of EC law; and will genuinely assist national court to make a judgement; but cannot be used merely to test the law or to delay the case.

Direct applicability
- Measure becomes part of national law without further enactment.
- So applies to Regulations but not to directives.

Direct effect:
- *Van Gend en Loos v Nederlands Administratie der Belastingin* accepted that certain measures should be enforceable by citizens of member states – if they were clear, precise and unconditional, and conferred rights on individuals;
- this is straightforward in the case of substantive Treaty Articles – *Reyners v Belgium*;
- and even in the case of decisions – *Grad v Finanzamt Traustein*;
- but not for directives which are not a complete legal instrument.

Direct effect of directives:
- *Van Duyn v Home Office* recognised that it would be incompatible with the binding nature of a directive in A429 if they could not be enforced;
- so provided that the date for implementation is passed – *Pubblico Ministero v Ratti*;
- they may be 'vertically' directly effective against the state itself – *Marshall v Southampton and SW Hampshire AHA (No 1)*;
- or an 'emanation of the state' – *Foster v British Gas plc*.

Indirect effect:
- *Von Colson and Kamann v Land Nordrhein-Westfalen* allows that since member states have an obligation under A10 to give full effect to EC law then they should interpret an improperly implemented directive so as to give effect to its objectives.

State liability:
- *Brasserie/Factortame* provides an action against states for failure to implement directives where the citizen suffers loss as a result.

5.1 SUPREMACY OF EC LAW

5.1.1 The reasons for the doctrine of supremacy

1. Supremacy has become:
   - the most entrenched; and
   - probably the least contested of EC principles.
2. It is essential that EC law should be uniformly applied.
3. Without 'supremacy' there could be no supranational context for the institutions, which would then have no effective power.
4. So, the real justifications for supremacy are:
   - the prevention of any questioning of the validity of EC law in member states.
   - the doctrine of 'preemption':
     (i) prevention of alternative legal interpretations of EC law by member state courts;
     (ii) prevention of enactment of conflicting legislating by member state governments.
5. However, the Treaties themselves make no reference to supremacy over all national law. The closest is Article 10 (the duty of loyalty): 'Member States shall take all appropriate measures ... to ensure fulfillment of the obligations arising out of this Treaty or resulting from actions taken by the institutions ... They shall abstain from any measure which could jeopardize the attainment of the objectives of the Treaty ...'. This has become a major tool in the hands of the ECJ.
6. Ultimately, the most logical basis for supremacy is the requirement of full integration. In any case economic integration would be virtually impossible if member states could deny and defy the supranational powers of the institutions.

5.1.2 The early statements of supremacy

1. The earliest definition of supremacy is in *26/62 Van Gend en Loos v The Commission*: 'The Community constitutes a new

legal order in international law, for whose benefits the states have limited their sovereign rights, albeit within limited fields …'.

2. The key effect of supremacy, then, is to limit the ability of member states to legislate contrary to EC law.

3. The definitive explanation comes in *6/64 Costa v ENEL*: 'By contrast with ordinary international treaties, the EEC Treaty has created its own legal system which on entry into force… became an integral part of the legal systems of the member states and which their courts are bound to apply … The transfer by member states from their national orders in favour of the Community order … carries with it a clear limitation of their sovereign right upon which a subsequent unilateral law, incompatible with the aims of the Community cannot prevail …'.

4. Three points clearly emerge:
   ● member states have given up certain of their sovereign powers to make law;
   ● member states and their citizens are bound by EC law;
   ● member states cannot unilaterally introduce conflicting law.

5. The ECJ has also declared that EC law cannot be invalidated even by national constitutional law – *International Handelsgesellschaft v EVGF 11/70*: 'Recourse to the legal rules or concepts of national law in order to judge the validity of measures adopted by the institutions … would have an adverse effect on the uniformity and efficacy of EC law. The validity of such measures can only be judged in the light of Community law…'.

6. So the ECJ has insisted that where EC law and national law conflict a court must give effect to the EC law – *Simmenthal SpA 106/77* 'the relationship between the provisions of the Treaty and directly applicable measures of the institutions on the one hand and national law … on the other… render automatically inapplicable any conflicting provision of current national law but … also preclude the valid adoption of new national legislative measures to the extent that they would be

incompatible with Community provisions ... every national court must ... apply Community law in its entirety ... and must accordingly set aside any provision of national law which may conflict with it whether prior or subsequent ...'.

7. Supremacy applies not only to directly conflicting national law, but to any contradictory law which encroaches on an area of Community competence (*Commission v France (The Merchant Sailor's case) 167/63*).

5.1.3 Continued development of the doctrine

1. The ECJ has continued to modify and expand the principle.
2. Another far reaching statement allowed national courts to set aside national legislation in areas of conflict – *R v Secretary of State for Transport ex parte Factortame No (2) C-213/89*: 'any legislative, administrative, or judicial practice which might impair the effectiveness of Community law by withholding from the national court ... the power to do everything necessary ... to set aside national legislative provisions which might prevent ... Community rules from having full force and effect are incompatible with those requirements which are the very essence of Community law ... the full effectiveness of Community law would be just as much impaired if a rule of national law could prevent a court ... from granting interim relief... It therefore follows that a court which ... would grant interim relief, if it were not for a rule of national law, is obliged to set aside that law...'.
3. The ECJ has also developed the principle that courts must interpret national legislation to comply with EC obligations, whether national law precedes or follows the conflicting EC law (*Von Colson v Land Nordrhein-Westfalen 14/83*, further developed by *Marleasing v La Commercial 106/89*).
4. The principle of liability towards citizens who suffer loss from a member state's breach of EC law also extends the doctrine of supremacy (*Francovich v Italy 6/90 and 9/90*).

5.1.4 Responses to supremacy by member states

1. Different states have responded in different ways.
2. Belgium and supremacy:
   - a monist state in respect of the international Treaty;
   - but EC law was incorporated by statute, so some early doubts on supremacy;
   - issue settled in *Minister for Economic Affairs v Fromagerie Franco-Suisse 'Le Ski'* (1972) – usual rule that a later statute repeals an earlier one could not apply to EC law, so EC law was supreme.
3. France and supremacy:
   - differences have occurred between civil appeal court views and administrative court (*Conseil d'Etat*);
   - civil courts have always accepted that EC law prevails over inconsistent cases and statute (*Von Kempis v Geldof* (1976));
   - but *Conseil d'Etat* has held that Directives cannot be used to challenge national administrative law *Minister for the Interior v Cohn Bendit* (1975);
   - though recently more prone to accept the principle.
4. Italy and supremacy:
   - takes a 'constructionist' approach – Italian law construed to be consistent with EC law;
   - the leading case is *Frontini* (1974): EC law is separate and superior and not within the scope of review of the Italian constitutional court.
5. UK and supremacy:
   - In the UK the focus has always been on interpretation of the EC Act 1972.
   - S2(1) gives force to EC law: 'All such rights, powers, liabilities, obligations and restrictions… created or arising by or under the Treaties, are without further enactment to be given legal effect …'.
   - Supremacy appears to be guaranteed by s2(4) which provides: '… any enactment passed or to be passed …

shall be construed and have effect subject to the foregoing provision of this section …'.

- Traditional argument has centred on whether it is an entrenched principle or merely a rule of construction.
- Judges have been willingly liberal in taking the latter view (*Garland v British Rail Engineering Ltd* (1979)).
- Judges have advocated a purposive approach to interpretation (*Pickstone v Freeman* (1988) and *Litster v Forth Dry Dock Co.* (1989)).
- However, in *Duke v Reliance GEC* (1988) Lord Templeman suggested that s2(4) does not permit an English court to 'distort a statute to enforce a Directive which has no direct effect between individuals…'.
- On Parliament's ability to deliberately oppose the EC, Lord Denning's view was: 'if…Parliament deliberately passes an Act with the intention of repudiating the Treaty or any provisions in it … and says so in express terms, then I would have thought that it would be the duty of our courts to follow the statute of our Parliament…' (*Macarthys v Smith 129/79*) – so ECA 1972 cannot be impliedly repealed though express repeal is theoretically retained.
- But acceptance of supremacy is now more clearly stated – Hoffman J in *Stoke-on-Trent v B and Q plc* (1990): 'The EC Treaty is the supreme law of the UK taking precedence over Acts of Parliament. Entry into the EC meant that Parliament surrendered its sovereign right to legislate contrary to the provisions of the Treaty … partial surrender of sovereignty was more than compensated for by the advantages of membership…'.
- And the definitive view of the meaning and scope of the 1972 Act is now Lord Bridge's in Factortame: '… whatever limitations of its sovereignty Parliament accepted when it enacted the EC Act 1972 was entirely voluntary. Under the terms of the 1972 Act it has always been clear that it is the duty of a UK court, when delivering final judgement, to override any rule of national law found to

be in conflict with any directly enforceable rule of
Community law…'.

5.2 DIRECT APPLICABILITY AND DIRECT EFFECT

5.2.1 Introduction

1. With supremacy, direct effect is another major element in ensuring the application of EC law in the member states.
2. It must be distinguished from direct applicability – A249 refers to certain community measures being either generally applicable or directly applicable.
3. The three are distinguished as follows:
   - general applicability merely means that the measure applies throughout the whole EU (so it would apply to a regulation but not to a decision);
   - direct applicability means that the measure becomes part of national law without need for further enactment (so it would apply to a regulation but not to a directive);
   - direct effect means that the measure creates rights and obligations which are enforceable in the national courts as well as in the ECJ (so it could easily apply to Treaty Articles and regulations, but is more problematic when applied to directives).
4. So there is a distinction between these last two:
   - directly applicable measures need not create justiciable rights e.g. a procedural regulation;
   - direct effect can exist without direct applicability, e.g. a Directive;
   - but a measure could be both.
5. Direct effect has been described as 'the first step in the judicial contribution to federalism…' (Craig: *Once upon a time in the west*).
6. It has also been described as 'a second principle of western jurisprudence to run alongside supremacy; namely the rule of law…' (Ian Ward: *A critical introduction to European law*).

7. Its most powerful justification is that it 'enhances the effectiveness or *effet utile* of binding norms of Community law ...' (Josephine Shaw: *Law of the European Union*, Palgrave).

8. It is the creation of the ECJ – its uncompromising nature has resulted in conflict with member states and in turn even more uncompromising principles, such as indirect effect.

5.2.2 The basic requirements for direct effect

1. The principle was first accepted by the ECJ in *Van Gend en Loos v Nederlands Administratie der Belastingen 26/62* 'Community law ... not only imposes obligations on individuals but is also intended to confer upon them rights which become part of their legal heritage. These rights are granted not only where they are expressly granted by the Treaty, but also by reason of obligations which the Treaty imposes in a clearly defined way upon individuals as well as upon member states and the institutions of the Community ...'.

2. So the ECJ accepted that since the Treaty was clearly intended to affect individuals as well as member states, it must be capable of creating rights which were enforceable by individuals.

3. The ECJ held that since A25 'contains a clear and unconditional prohibition ... it [is] ideally adapted to produce direct effects between member states and their subjects ...'.

4. By *Van Gend en Loos* direct effect only applied to 'stand still Articles':
   ● but this limitation soon disappeared;
   ● and a variety of provisions have since been held to be directly effective;
   ● though there are still measures which remain unenforceable if worded in conditional terms.

5. The requirements for direct effect have been modified by the case law, e.g. *Reyner v Belgium 2/74* and are: the provision

must be clear, precise and unconditional and non-dependent.

6. *Van Gend en Loos* concerned a Treaty Article that conferred rights, but the principle of direct effect has been extended to other EC law by the case law.

5.2.3 The basic distinction between vertical and horizontal direct effect

1. The ECJ has also been responsible for helping to identify the principles of vertical and horizontal direct effect and clarifying the distinctions between them.

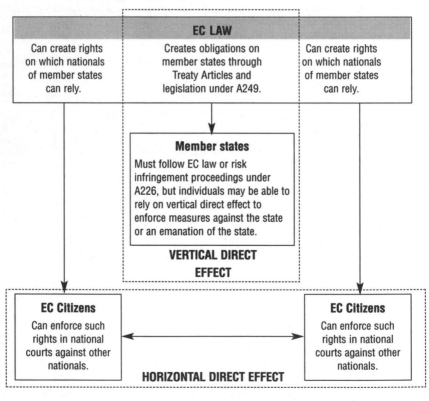

The differences between vertical and horizontal direct effect

2. The distinction can be critical in determining whether a person can enforce EC law in a national court.
3. Vertical direct effect concerns the relationship between EC law and the national law:
   - measures of EC law create obligations on the state;
   - so failure to honour such obligations would normally result in A226 action;
   - but it can also mean that an individual can rely on the measures in an action against the state;
   - this was the case in both *Van Duyn v Home Office 41/74* and *Pubblico Ministero v Ratti 148/78*, which were both fought against government departments;
   - the concept has been extended to include bodies that are 'emanations of the state' (public bodies) and so may extend rights to certain individuals.
4. Horizontal direct effect, on the other hand, is precisely about the relationship between individuals, so concerns rights enforceable in national courts.

5.2.4 Direct effect and Treaty Articles

1. Direct effect was first accepted in *Van Gend en Loos*.
2. However, the principle test for application now is that laid down in *Reyners v Belgium 2/74*.
3. Directly effective Treaty Articles could include:
   - 'stand still' Articles, e.g. *Van Gend en Loos* and A25;
   - originally also included Articles imposing a duty on the state to act, e.g. *Eunomia 18/71* and the since repealed A16;
   - Articles that give rights to individuals, e.g. *Van Duyn v Home Office 41/74* and A39; *Reyners v Belgium 2/74* and A43; *Defrenne v SABENA 43/75* and A141.

5.2.5 Direct Effect and Regulations

1. Regulations create obligations without need for further enactment because they are of 'general application' and are

'directly applicable'.

2. So they will usually be directly effective, subject to *Reyners* test (*Leonesio v Ministero dell'Agricoltora and delle Foreste 93/71 (The widow Leonesio)*).

3. But a Regulation may not be directly effective if too vague.

5.2.6 Direct effect and decisions

1. A decision by A249 is 'binding in its entirety on the party to whom it is addressed'.

2. So it would be 'incompatible with the binding nature of decisions to exclude the possibility of direct effect...' (*Grad v Finanzamt Traustein 9/70*).

3. It is less certain whether a decision addressed to a member state could have horizontal effect.

5.2.7 Direct effect and directives

1. By A249, directives are 'binding as to the result to be achieved':
   - so they are seen as creating an obligation on member states to pass law to achieve the objective;
   - but not as automatically creating substantive rights for citizens to enforce, because they fail the *Van Gend* test – they are dependent.

2. The ECJ was prepared to overlook this limitation in *Van Duyn v Home Office*:
   - because 'it would be incompatible with the binding effect attributed to a Directive by (A249) to exclude, in principle, the possibility that the obligation which it imposes may be invoked by those concerned ...';
   - so a directive can be enforced provided that the three criteria for direct effect are met.

3. But only where the time limit for implementation has passed (*Pubblico Ministero v Ratti 148/78*).

4. Also, a directive can be vertically but not horizontally effective

(*Marshall v Southampton and South West Hampshire AHA (Teaching) (No 1) 152/84*).

5. Where the directive is properly implemented there would be national law and so need to use direct effect. An unimplemented directive can only be relied on as against the state, e.g.:

- pre-privatised British Gas (*Foster v British Gas plc 188/89*); tax authorities (*Becker 8/81*); and the police (*Johnston v The Royal Ulster Constabulary 222/84*);
- but not a publicly owned manufacturing company (*Rolls Royce plc v Doughty* (1987));
- the test in *Foster* and also in *Griffin v South West Water* (1995) is whether:
  - (i) the body provides a public service;
  - (ii) the body is under the control of the state;
  - (iii) the body exercises special powers;
- so this creates major anomalies in the case of private bodies (*Duke v Reliance GCE* (1988)), against whom an unimplemented directive cannot be enforced.

6. A directive can be referred to after implementation to ensure its objectives are achieved *Verbond v Nederlands Ondernemingen 51/76*

5.2.8 Indirect Effect

1. As a result of the limitations of using vertical direct effect, the ECJ has used the obligation under A10 to conform with and give effect to EC law (irrespective of whether or not it is directly effective) to develop the principle of indirect effect (the *Von Colson* principle), which applies to all EC law, not just directives.

2. As the court said in *Von Colson and Kamann v Land Nordrhein-Westfalen 14/83*, 'Since the duty under [A10] to ensure fulfillment of (an) obligation was binding on all national courts ... it follows that ... courts are required to interpret their national law in the light of the wording and purpose of the directive ...'.

3. The ECJ in *Von Colson* ignored the horizontal/vertical issue, and direct effect generally:
   - it was left ambiguous to which national law indirect effect would apply so, for example, HL refused to apply it in *Duke*;
   - it was also left ambiguous how far national courts should go to ensure conformity of national law and EC law.
4. However, these problems seem to have been resolved by *Marleasing SA v La Commercial Internacional de Alimentacion c-106/89*:
   - the ECJ held that the obligation to conform applied 'whether the provisions concerned pre-date or post-date the directive …';
   - so its scope in *Marleasing* is potentially very wide, with consequences for precedent and statutory interpretation;
   - although there does seem to be a difference between the *Von Colson* approach (to do 'everything possible' to achieve conformity), and the *Simmenthal* approach (to do 'everything necessary');
   - the ECJ already seems to have linked the concepts of direct and indirect effect (*Johnston v Chief Constable of the RUC 222/84*).

5.2.9 State liability for failure to implement

1. The third way to avoid the problems of direct effect and directives came in *Francovich v Italy 6/90 and 9/90*:
   - the ECJ held that 'the full effectiveness of EC provisions … and the rights they recognise would be undermined if individuals were unable to recover damages where their rights were infringed by a breach of EC law attributable to a member state …';
   - so citizens should be able to sue the state for non-implementation of a directive.
2. The conditions for liability are:
   - the directive must confer rights for individuals – the contents of which must be identifiable in the wording;

- there must be a causal link between the damage suffered and the failure to implement the directive;
- and the cases of *Brasserie du Pecheur SA v Germany* and *R v Secretary of State for Transport, ex parte Factortame 46 and 48/93* have added another – that the breach by the member state is sufficiently serious (*Dillenkofer v Federal Republic of Germany C-178/94* suggests that non-implementation is sufficiently serious).

3. The *Francovich* principle is the most far reaching so far and has several implications:
   - it conflicts with national rules on non-implementation;
   - but the need to show direct effect is removed;
   - as is the strained construction of national law through indirect effect;
   - it focuses instead on the duty of the member state to implement EC law and attaches rigorous sanctions for failure to implement;
   - so it removes any advantage of non-implementation.

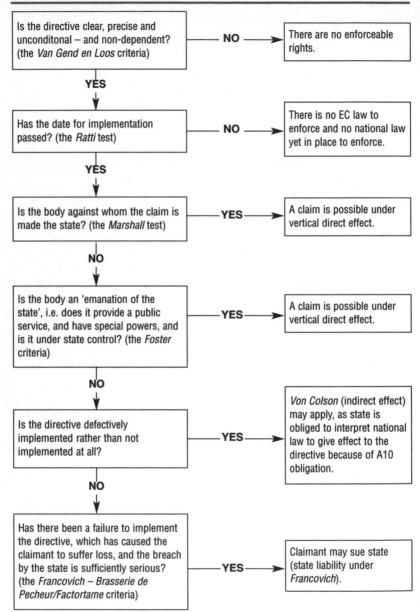

The possible enforceability of directives

5.3 A234 REFERENCES AND PRELIMINARY RULINGS

5.3.1 Introduction

1. Reference procedure is critical to both supremacy and direct effect, because it is the means of ensuring uniform application of the law.

2. The ethos of reference procedure is:
- to create a collaborative bond between EC and the national courts;
- to recognise that national courts are ultimately the best equipped to give effect to EC law;
- to demonstrate that EC law is part of national law.

3. 'The grand objectives of a Community legal order which include the intermeshing of Community law and national law, could not be achieved without some organic mechanism for ensuring the uniform application of EC law ... the ECJ frequently reminds us that (this) is the purpose of A234 ...' (Josephine Shaw, *Law of the European Union*, Palgrave)

4. It provides a means for national courts to be guided on 'meaning or validity' of EC law in a case depending on EC law.

5. It accounts for the largest area of ECJ work, and for most of the crucially important decisions.

5.3.2 The scope of the A234 procedure

1. Under A234(1), as amended by the TEU, the ECJ has jurisdiction to give preliminary rulings on:
- the interpretation of the EC Treaty;
- validity and interpretation of acts of Community institutions (and now also of the Central Bank).

2. So the ECJ clearly has jurisdiction to interpret all Treaty Articles and the acts of the institutions, which are clearly those in A249: Regulations, Directives, and Decisions.

3. The ECJ has no jurisdiction to interpret national law.
4. By A234(2), 'Where such a question is raised before any court or tribunal of a member state… [it] may, if it considers a decision on the question is necessary to enable it to give judgement, request the Court of Justice to give a ruling…'.
5. By A234(3), 'Where any such question is raised in a case pending before a court or tribunal of a member state, against whose decisions there is no judicial remedy under national law, that court or tribunal shall bring the matter before the Court of Justice'.

5.3.3 The meaning of 'any court or tribunal'

1. This may include 'the whole range of bodies which embody the judicial power of the state regardless of what they are called…'.
2. The key elements are that the body:
   ● must be recognised in the national judicial system;
   ● must be a permanent body;
   ● must exercise a judicial function;
   ● must give a decision according to the rule of law.
3. Examples of bodies falling within A234 procedure include:
   ● *Vaassen 61/65*, a Dutch Social Security Tribunal for migrant workers;
   ● *Broeckmeuler 246/80*, a Dutch GP's Registration Appeals Committee;
   ● *Pretore di Salo v X 14/86*, preliminary enquiries by a Magistrate;
   ● in the UK it has included Employment Tribunals, the EAT and Social Security Tribunals.
4. Examples of bodies not within the scope of A234 include:
   ● *Borker 138/80*, the Paris Bar Council
   ● *Nordsee Hochseefischerei GmbH v Reederei Mond 102/81*, commercial arbitration.

5.3.4 Paragraph 2 and the discretion to refer

1. Paragraph 2 and paragraph 3 identify two different situations:
   - discretionary referral – from the word 'may' in 2;
   - mandatory referral – from the word 'shall' in 3.
2. By paragraph 2 courts have discretion to refer where they feel it is 'necessary'.
3. A national court will find it necessary when it requires an ECJ ruling in order to be able to give judgement.
4. The ECJ has developed its own test, in *CILFIT 283/81*, of when a reference is not necessary:
   - where EC law is irrelevant or peripheral to the issue;
   - where there is an existing interpretation – the principle of *acte clair* applies (see *Procureur dela Republique v Chiron 271/84 and274/81*);
   - where correct interpretation is so obvious that there can be no doubt.
5. UK courts have also drawn up their own guidelines:
   - *Lord Denning in Bulmer v Bollinger* (1974) – before referring judge must be sure:
     - (i) EC law would be conclusive of the case;
     - (ii) there is no previous ECJ ruling;
     - (iii) the doctrine of *acte clare* does not apply;
     - (iv) the facts of the case are already decided;
     - (v) delay caused by reference is not unwarranted.
   - though these guidelines have been criticised for being too negative. A more positive approach is Bingham J in *Commissioners of Customs and Excise v Samex SpA* (1983) – the ECJ is better to interpret EC law because:
     - (i) it scrutinises all the language versions;
     - (ii) it oversees EC law in total;
     - (iii) it has a better understanding of purposive interpretation.

5.3.5 Paragraph 3 and the obligation to refer

1. This is known as the 'compulsory reference' procedure –

strangely as there is much controversy surrounding when it will apply.

2. One view is that only courts of last resort are covered, e.g. HL in the UK.

3. But another view is that it includes any court where the right to appeal is denied for whatever reasons, e.g. in *Costa v ENEL* the reference was made by a *guidice concilliatore* (an Italian Magistrate).

4. The position is very unsettled in the UK courts, e.g. see CA and *R v Henn and Darby* (1978) and the High Court, and *Magnavision NV v General Optical Council (No 2)* (1987).

5. In general the risk of the 'floodgates' being opened seems to suggest that the strict meaning of paragraph 3 is compromised for the *CILFIT* criteria.

6. However, failure by a court of last resort to refer can result in an A226 action against the member state.

5.3.6 The limitations on making references

1. These were stated in *Foglia v Novella (No 1) 104/79 and (No 2) 244/80*:
   - reference must involve a genuine issue of EC law;
   - reference will genuinely assist a national court to make a judgement;
   - reference may not be used to give opinions on hypothetical situations in order to merely test the law;
   - nor can a party merely use it as a delaying tactic;
   - in these last two situations a reference will be refused

2. The reference must be 'necessary'.

3. Only the ECJ has authority to declare provisions of EC law invalid – to prevent damaging uniform application of EC law would *Firma Foto-Frost v Hauptzollampt Lubeck 314/85*.

5.3.7 The effect of preliminary ruling under A234

1. There is nothing specific in the Treaty to indicate what the effect will be.

2. However, under A5 it is clear that member state courts are bound to decide cases in accordance with ECJ case law.

3. The ECJ has its own case law on the subject, suggesting that in a case where a reference has been made the ruling is binding on the national court (*Milch-Fett-und Eierkontor v HZA Saarbrucker 29/68*).

4. Though it is the interpretation of law which is binding – there is no question of *res judicita* applying.

CHAPTER 6

INTRODUCTION TO THE LAW OF THE INTERNAL MARKET

6.1 THE AIMS OF THE SINGLE MARKET

1. The internal market is a system of regional economic and social integration – a large trading unit in which there are no internal barriers to trade.
2. The internal market also aims towards monetary unity and political integration that will secure not only the economic welfare of the citizens of European states, but will also secure peace.

6.2 THE FOUR FREEDOMS

1. The logic of the founding Treaties was to create a single market, removing trade barriers based on national discrimination.
2. Hence the four freedoms:
   - free movement of workers;
   - freedom to provide services;
   - free movement of capital;
   - free movement of goods.
3. Social mobility is ensured through A39 for workers, A43 for businesses or professions, and A49 for providing services.
4. The purpose is to ensure that member states do nothing to unfairly favour national enterprises and discriminate.
5. Free movement of goods is achieved in numerous ways:
   - by prohibiting customs duties on imports and exports, and all other charges having equivalent effect (A25);
   - by prohibiting discriminatory taxation (A90);

- by prohibiting quantitative restrictions (quotas) on imports and measures having equivalent effect (A28) and on exports (A29); exemptions exist in A30.

6. A Common Customs Tariff in A23 is governed by A26 and A27.

7. Goods are not defined in the Treaty, but have been defined as 'anything capable of money valuation and of being the object of commercial transactions ...' (*Commission v Italy Re Export Tax on Art Treasures 7/68*).

CHAPTER 7

A28 AND A29 FREE MOVEMENT OF GOODS

Prohibitions on quantitative restrictions – A28 and imports:

- Not defined in Treaty but is in case law – measures that amount to a total or partial restraint on imports, exports or goods in transit.
- So could include quota (*Salgoil SpA v Italian Minister of Trade*) or a complete ban on imports (*R v Henn & Darby*).
- Prohibited by A28.

A29 and exports:
- ECJ takes a different approach.
- A29 only restricts measures meant to differentiate between domestic and export trade and help exports at expense of other states (*Groenveld BV v Produktschap voor Veer en Viees*).

Measures having equivalent effect (MEQRs):

- Not defined in Treaty, but in *Procureur du Roi v Dassonville* – all trading rules enacted by member states which are capable of hindering, directly or indirectly, actually or potentially, intra-Community trade are to be considered as measures having an effect equivalent to quantitative restrictions – and are prohibited.
- But must distinguish between distinctly applicable (affects only imports) and indistinctly applicable (applies to imports and domestic goods – but affects imports disproportionately).
- But does not apply to selling arrangements if equally applied to imports and domestic goods (*Keck and Mithouard*).

FREE MOVEMENT OF GOODS

A30 derogations:
- Exemptions possible for public morality, public policy, or public security; protection of health of humans, animals or plants; protection of industrial and commercial property.
- List is exhaustive and narrower than *Cassis*.
- A30 can only be used if the measure is proportionate to the objective to be achieved, and non-arbitrary.
- Can only apply A30 to extent measure concerned is necessary to achieve objective – no further.
- Public morality varies by state (*R v Henn and Darby*).
- Public security only appropriate in crisis (*Campus Oil*).
- Public health must involve real risk to health (*Commission v UK (French Turkeys)*).

Cassis de Dijon principle:
- Principle in (*Cassis de Dijon case*) *Rewe-Zentral AG v Bundesmono-polverwaltung fur Branntwein*.
- Only applies to indistinctly applicable measures.
- Restriction lawful if to satisfy mandatory requirements for effective tax, protection of public health, fairness of commercial transactions or consumer protection – and proportionate.
- Second test – if product lawfully produced and marketed in one member state then should be able to circulate freely throughout Community.

7.1 PROHIBITIONS ON QUANTITATIVE RESTRICTIONS ON IMPORTS (A28), AND EXPORTS (A29), AND MEASURES HAVING EQUIVALENT EFFECT

1. A quantitative restriction is a national measure that restricts the volume or amount of imports or exports, not by artificially raising the costs of importing or exports (as would be the case with a tariff or a tax), but by placing direct or indirect limits on the physical quantity of imports or exports that may enter or leave the market.

2. The most common form of quantitative restriction is a quota:
   - Outright bans on trade are also possible.
   - There are examples, despite the prohibition (*Commission v UK (Re imports of Dutch potatoes)* (1979); *Commission v France (Re sheepmeat from UK)* (1979); *Commission v UK (Re imports of UHT milk)* (1983).

3. The Treaty deals with quantitative restrictions in:
   - A28 in the case of imports;
   - A29 in the case of exports;
   - A30 which provides exemptions from the prohibitions if certain justifications are shown.

4. Quantitative restrictions are not defined in the Treaty:
   - but they are in the case law: 'measures which amount to a total or partial restraint on imports, exports or goods in transit …';
   - so have included, for example:
     (i) quotas (*Salgoil SpA v Italian Minister of Trade 13/68*);
     (ii) a ban on importing pornographic material (*R v Henn & Darby 34/79*).

7.2 MEASURES HAVING EQUIVALENT EFFECT (MEQR)

1. 'Measures having equivalent effect to a quantitative restriction' (MEQR) are not defined in the Treaty, but have been widely

interpreted (*Commission v Ireland (Re discriminatory promotional policies) 249/81*).

2. Directive 70/50 was issued to provide some explanation on what measures can be equivalent to a quantitative restriction:
   * distinctly applicable measures – those that apply only to imported goods and which make importing goods more difficult than using domestic products;
   * indistinctly applicable measures – those that are equally applicable to imported and domestic goods, which only contravene A28 if their restrictive effect exceeds the effect intrinsic to trade rules.

3. Practices identified under the Directive have included:
   * measures designed to specify less favourable prices for imports than for domestic products;
   * practices establishing minimum and maximum prices below or above which imports are prohibited or reduced;
   * standards subjecting imports to conditions relating to shape, size, weight or composition which cause them to suffer in competition with domestic products;
   * laws restricting marketing of imported products in the absence of an agent/representative in the importing state.

4. But the classic early definition was that in the *Dassonville* formula: 'All trading rules enacted by member states which are capable of hindering, directly or indirectly, actually or potentially, intra-Community trade are to be considered as measures having an effect equivalent to quantitative restrictions ...' (*Procureur du Roi v Dassonville 8/74*).

5. *Dassonville* has been followed *Tasca 65/75* and *Van Tiggle 82/77*.

7.3 A30 AND THE DEROGATIONS FROM A28 AND A29

1. A30 provides derogations where 'justified on grounds of public morality, public policy, or public security; the protection of health and life of humans, animals or plants; the protection of national treasures possessing artistic, historic or

archaeological value; or the protection of industrial and commercial property ... prohibitions and restrictions shall not, however, constitute a means of arbitrary discrimination or a disguised restriction on trade between member states ...'.

2. So three key points stand out:
   - the list of exemptions under A30 is exhaustive (and is also narrower than *Cassis*);
   - as a result, A30 must be construed strictly and narrowly;
   - member states may claim exemptions under A30 only to the extent that the measure concerned is justified (necessary) to achieve the objective, and no further.

3. So, inevitably situations arise where the ECJ will not apply A30 (*Commission v Ireland 113/80*).

4. The ECJ has struggled to produce a truly Community interpretation of public morality since moral perceptions vary from state to state (*R v Henn and Darby 34/79*).

5. Cases where public morality was used as an A30 derogation include *Conegate Ltd v Customs and Excise Commissioners 121/85* and *Quietlynn v Southend BC c-23/89*.

6. On public policy too, the ECJ has interpreted strictly but without achieving a Community concept (*Commission v Germany 12/74 (the Sekt case)*), and the ground has only been successfully used once (*R v Thompson and Others 7/78*).

7. Public security is only likely to be successfully claimed in relation to a crisis (*Campus Oil 72/83*).

8. Protecting the health and life of humans, animals and plants is a straightforward public health exception:
   - The range of measures where a breach of A28 may occur includes: import bans, licensing systems, inspections (particularly cross-border), prior authorisations, etc., any of which might be considered to be MEQRs (*Commission v UK (UHT Milk) 124/81*).
   - But a real risk to health must be involved (*Commission v UK (French Turkeys) 40/82*).
   - A30 can only apply if the measures are proportionate to the objectives to be achieved and protection of health cannot be achieved by other measures (*Commission v*

France (Re Italian Table Wines) 42/82, but see also *Officier Van Justitie v Sandoz BV 174/82*, where a prohibition on an additive was allowed because there was no general medical consensus).

● The real problem is the subjective character of analysing the real reasons for the restriction (*R v Secretary of State for the Home Department ex parte Evans Medical and Macfarlane Smith c-324/93*).

● Failure of other states to operate according to recommendations but complying with a directive will not allow a state to rely on A30 (*R v Minister of Agriculture Fisheries and Food ex parte Compassion in World Farming Ltd c-1/96* (19th March 1998)).

9. Protection of national treasures is a very precise area of justification, not yet successfully argued (*Commission v Italy (Re Export Tax on Art Treasures) 7/68*).

10. Protection of industrial and commercial property is, in effect, the intellectual property law of the EC and a giant area in its own right.

11. But A30 has been used as a defence against national regulatory rules (*Torfaen BC v B and Q plc 145/88*).

7.4 THE CASSIS DE DIJON PRINCIPLE

1. Subsequently interpretation of A28 came about in the *Cassis de Dijon* principle: 'Obstacles to movement within EC arising from disparities between national laws relating to the marketing of the product in question must be accepted in so far as those provisions may be recognised as necessary in order to satisfy the mandatory requirements relating in particular to the effectiveness of fiscal supervision, the protection of public health, the fairness of commercial transactions and the defence of the consumer...', *Rewe -Zentral AG v Bundesmonopolverwaltung fur Branntwein 120/78 (The Cassis de Dijon case)*.

2. It is important because it removed the assumption that A28 only applied where discrimination between imported and domestic products could be shown.
3. So the principle mitigated the harshness of the *Dassonville* principle so that reference to A30 is not always necessary:
   - providing the measure was necessary (*Miro BV 182/84*);
   - or for public protection (*Duphar BV v Netherlands 238/82*);
   - and was proportionate for the objective to be achieved.
4. A second rule in the case was that if a product was lawfully produced and marketed in one member state then it should be able to circulate freely throughout the Community (since clarified by the Commission), but this can be rebutted (*Commission v Germany 174/84 (German Beer purity)*).
5. However, the ECJ has also recognised that A28 has been used too often in attempts only to subvert national law which has no effect on imports (*Keck and Mithouard c-267/91 and 268/91 (joined cases)*, where the ECJ held that the *Cassis de Dijon* principle will not apply to selling arrangements, providing that these were applied equally to domestic and imported products so that imports were not discriminated against).

7.5 A29 AND EXPORTS

1. The ECJ takes a different approach to exports and A29.
2. Originally the *Dassonville* formula was assumed to apply.
3. But the ECJ has ruled that A29 only restricts measures that are designed to differentiate between the domestic and export trade of a member state so as to confer a benefit on exports at the expense of other states (*Groenveld BV v Produktschap voor Veer en Vlees 15/79*).
4. So, measures applying equally to domestic products for the national market and those for export do not offend A29 (*Oebel 155/80*).
5. However, direct discrimination involving distinctly applicable measures does (*Bouhelier 53/76*).

CHAPTER 8

A25 AND CUSTOMS TARIFFS, AND A90 AND DISCRIMINATORY TAXATION

A25 and prohibitions on customs duties and measures having equivalent effect:
- Introduced to prevent member states from subverting the single market by use of customs duties.
- A25 is directly effective (*Van Gend en Loos v Nederlandse Administratie des Belastingen*).
- The ECJ provides definition of MEQR – 'any pecuniary charge … imposed unilaterally on domestic or foreign goods [because] they cross a frontier and which is not a customs duty' (*Commission v Italy* and *Simmenthal v Italian Minister for Finance*).
- So, a disguised charge may be invalid (*Social Fonds voor de Diamantarbeiders*.

A25 AND CUSTOMS DUTIES
A90 AND DISCRIMINATORY TAXATION

A90 and prohibitions on discriminatory taxation:
- Two aspects to A90:
  - (i) no member states should impose, directly or indirectly, on products of other member states internal taxation in excess of that imposed on similar domestic products;
  - (ii) no member states should impose an internal tax of such a nature to give protection to domestic products.
- To breach A90 the tax must discriminate against imports, e.g. applying sliding scales (*Humbold v Directeur des Services Fiscaux*) or only applying tax to imports (*Bobie v HZA Aachen-Nord*).

8.1 A25 AND PROHIBITION ON CUSTOMS DUTIES AND CHARGES HAVING EQUIVALENT EFFECT

1. Customs duties are a very old device of protectionism.

2. So they were one of first mechanisms for the Treaty to attack.

3. To prevent member states subverting the Treaties by introducing measures not called customs duties but with the same effect, the EC Treaty prohibited any such measures.

4. Ex A14-A15 removed all tariff barriers in transitional period.

5. A25 itself is a 'stand still' article prohibiting the introduction of any customs duties or provision having equivalent effect.

6. A25 is also directly effective, so as to be enforceable by citizens (*Van Gend en Loos v Nederlandse Administratie des Belastingen 26/62*).

7. Measures having equivalent effect (MEQRs) are more problematic and not defined in the Treaty:

   * so a definition is given by ECJ case law: 'any pecuniary charge ... imposed unilaterally on domestic or foreign goods (because) they cross a frontier and which is not a customs duty in the strict sense constitutes a charge having equivalent effect ... even if it is not imposed for the benefit of the state ...' (*Commission v Italy 24/68*);

   * reiterated in *Simmenthal v Italian Minister for Finance 35/76* and *Bauhuis v Netherlands State 46/76*.

8. So, a disguised charge may be an obstacle to trade and thus have equivalent effect and be invalid (*Social Fonds voor de Diamantarbeiders 2/69* and *3/69*).

9. But a genuine tax will not, if within the requirements of A90.

10. A levy on services is permissible if:

   * the cost is proportionate to the service received;

   * it is in accordance with EC requirements;

   * there is no discrimination between domestic and other EC goods (compare *Bauhuis v Netherlands 46/76* with *Commission v Belgium 132/82*).

8.2 A90 AND DISCRIMINATORY TAXATION

1. Internal taxes may distort trade if differently applied:
   * not preventing free movement but as a disincentive;
   * more favourable tax regimes can have the same effect.
2. There are two aspects to A90:
   * no member states should impose, directly or indirectly, on the products of other member states' internal taxation in excess of that imposed on similar domestic products;
   * no member states should impose an internal tax of such a nature to give protection to domestic products.
3. But they should be construed as a whole, not separately (*Fazenda Publica v Americo c-345/93*).
4. Direct taxation is generally taken to refer to income tax, etc.:
   * so A90 applies to indirect taxes;
   * and means adopted to harmonise taxes include VAT.
5. 'Internal taxation' is interpreted broadly, so might include:
   * charges levied as a percentage of imported products, not general tax (*Llanelli v Meroni 74/76*);
   * but can take account of, for example, higher cost of domestic raw materials (*Luxembourg v Belgium 2/62* and *3/62*);
   * higher manufacturing costs (*Commission v Italy 28/69*).
6. Similar products are not defined in the Treaty but in case law:
   * the ECJ tends to view similarity in terms of way viewed by consumer rather than actual or potential use (*John Walker v Ministeriet for Skatter 243/86*);
   * tax may be discriminatory if products are not so similar in character but do compete (*Commission v UK 170/78*).
7. Taxation must discriminate against imported products to offend A90:
   * will do so particularly if sliding scales are applied (*Humblot v Directeur des Services Fiscaux 112/84*);
   * and where imports but not domestic products are subject to fixed scales (*Bobie v HZA Aachen-Nord 127/75*).

CHAPTER 9

A39 AND THE FREE MOVEMENT OF WORKERS

Definition of worker:
- pursuit of effective and genuine activity (*Levin v Staatsecretaris van Justitie*);
- performs service in return for remuneration (*Lawrie-Blum v Land Baden-Wurttemberg*);
- worker who has lost job but is capable of finding other work (*Hoekstra*);
- part-timer needing supplementary benefit (*Kempf v Staatsecretaris voor Justitie*);
- no formal wage but involved in economic activity (*Steymann v Statsecretaris voor Justitie*);
- person looking for work (*R v Immigration Appeal Tribunal ex parte Antonissen*);
- but not if not for a genuine reason (*Bettray v Staatsecretaris van Justitie*).

FREE MOVEMENT OF WORKERS

Limitations on free movement
- A39(3) and Directive 64/221 allow derogations for public policy, public security, public health.
- Public policy for genuine threat to society (*R v Bouchereau*).
- But not if not illegal in host state (*Adoui & Cornaille v Belgium*).
- Public policy or security must be exclusively on conduct of individual concerned (*Van Duyn v The Home Office*).
- Public health lists prescribed diseases, e.g. TB.
- A39(4) permits limiting access to public service on nationality.
- Applies only to civil authority or security of state (*Commission v Belgium*).

Rights of entry and residence
- Directive 68/360 – can leave home state to seek employment in another state and enter on production of valid identity card or passport, and get residence permit with relevant documents;
- can enter and look for work (*Proceurer de Roi v Royer*);
- for at least 6 months (*R v Immigration Appeal Tribunal ex parte Antonissen*).

Equal treatment:
Regulation 1612/68 demands equal treatment in all employment matters, including:
- no limiting offers of employment or number of migrant workers (*Commission v France (Re French Merchant Seamen)*);
- linguistic tests are valid (*Groener v Minister of Education*);
- equal conditions for nationals and migrants in pay, conditions, dismissals (*Wurttembergische Milchvertung-Sudmilch A.G. v Ugliola*);
- dependenats have rights to live with worker irrespective of nationality (*Lebon*).

Rights of families:
- Regulation 1612/68 gives right to spouses, dependants under 21, and ascendant relatives, and sometimes even cohabitees (*Netherlands State v Anne florence Reed*).

Right to remain after employment:
- Regulation 1251/70 gives right to remain permanently to retired workers, incapacitated workers, frontier workers, and family if worker dies during employment.

9.1 INTRODUCTION

1. This was essential to the creation of the common market.
2. The EC Treaty required 'abolition, between member states, of obstacles to free movement of persons and services …'.
3. The basis for free movement was in A6 'any discrimination on grounds of nationality shall be prohibited …'.
4. Found in A39–A42 and regulations and directives.
5. Equivalent rights exist in A43 and A49 for establishment of services.

9.2 THE CHARACTER AND EXTENT OF A39

1. Member states were required to abolish any discrimination between workers of different states based on nationality.
2. Member states were required to apply equality to employment, remuneration and all other conditions of employment, e.g. the same for migrant workers as for workers of the host nation.
3. A state can derogate on public security, public health, or public policy grounds, and exclude from public service.
4. The extent of the right is:
   - to take up offers of work already made;
   - to move freely throughout EU to seek employment;
   - to remain in a member state for employment under the same conditions as a national of the member state;
   - to remain after employment.

9.3 THE DEFINITION OF WORKER

1. A39 applies to 'workers', but no definition is provided.
2. So, definition comes from numerous A234 references.
3. Citizenship under TEU is not the same as a worker.
4. The earliest definition held A39 applied only to 'the pursuit of effective and genuine activities to the exclusion of activities

of such a small scale as to be regarded as purely marginal and ancillary ...' (*Levin v Staatsecretaris van Justitie 53/81*).

5. Essential characteristics of a worker are 'performance of services, under the direction of another, in return for remuneration, for a certain period of time ...' (*Lawrie-Blum v Land Baden-Wurttemberg 66/85*).

6. The ECJ has interpreted the definition of worker liberally:
   - a worker who has lost his job but is capable of finding other work (*Hoekstra v Bestuur der Badrijfsvereniging voor Detailhandel en Ambachten 75/63*);
   - a part-timer needing supplementary benefit for subsistence (*Kempf v Staatsecretaris voor Justitie 139/85*);
   - a person with no formal wage but involved in an economic activity (*Steymann v Statsecretaris voor Justitie 196/87*);
   - a professional sportsman (*Dona v Mantero 13/76*);
   - a person looking for work (*R v Immigration Appeal Tribunal ex parte Antonissen 292/89*).

7. However, the ECJ has also imposed limitations:
   - where there is no economic purpose to the activity (*Bettray v Staatsecretaris van Justitie 344/87*);
   - if the sport is not a genuine economic activity (*Walrave & Koch v Association Union Cycliste Internationale 36/74*).

9.4 RIGHTS OF WORKERS' FAMILIES

1. A39 gives rights to workers' families – defined in regulation 1612/68 as spouse and dependants under 21 and in ascendant line of worker or spouse (nationality irrelevant).

2. Sometimes rights extend to cohabitees (*Netherlands state v Anne Florence Reed 59/85*).

3. Rights are not lost through mere separation (*Diatta v Land Berlin 267/83*).

4. But may be with complete marital breakdown (*R Secretary of State for the Home Department ex parte Sandhu (1985)*).

9.5 RIGHTS OF ENTRY AND RESIDENCE

1. These rights are identified in directive 68/360:
   - to leave home state to seek employment in another state;
   - to enter another state 'on production of a valid identity card or passport ...' (non-EU nationals need visas);
   - to obtain a residence permit by producing relevant documents.
2. Residence permits must be renewable, for five years minimum, and not withdrawn for illness or involuntary unemployment.
3. The right includes to enter and look for work (*Proceurer de Roi v Royer 48/75*).
4. There is no fixed time limit, but six months has been held sufficient, justifying removal if past (*R v Immigration Appeal Tribunal ex parte Antonissen C-292/89*) (three months in *Royer*).
5. Failures to observe formalities do not justify refusal to allow entry or residence (*R v Pieck 157/79*).
6. Nor do they justify deportation (*Watson & Bellman 118/75*).
7. Seasonal workers are allowed temporary residence permits.

9.6 THE RIGHT TO EQUAL TREATMENT

1. A39 requires abolition of discrimination on nationality in employment, remuneration and conditions.
2. Regulation 1612/68 requires equal treatment in all employment matters and elimination of obstacles to mobility. It has three Titles:
   - Title I – eligibility for employment:
     (i) A3 prohibits limiting offers of employment or restricting numbers of migrant workers (*Commission v France (Re French Merchant Seamen) 167/73*);
     (ii) A5 no discriminatory tests for recruitment, e.g. vocational, medical or other;

(iii) linguistic tests are valid (*Groener v Minister of Education 378/87*).

- Title II – equality in conditions of employment:
  (i) A7(1) ensures equal conditions for nationals and migrants in pay, conditions, dismissals, etc. (*Wurttembergische Milchvertung-Sudmilch A.G. v Ugliola 15/69* and *Sotgiu v Deutsche Bundepost 152/73*);
  (ii) by A7(2) migrants should receive the same tax and social advantages as nationals (*de Fer Francais 32/75*);
  (iii) the right exists whether or not linked to a contract of employment (*Ministere Public v Even 207/78*);
  (iv) social advantage can include, for example, a grant (*Brown 197/86*).
- Title III – workers' families.
  (i) A10(1) gives family, if dependants, rights to live with worker irrespective of their nationality (*Lebon 316/85*);
  (ii) A11 gives the right to take employment regardless of nationality (*Gul 131/85*);
  (iii) A12 gives workers' children the same rights as nationals to education, training and apprenticeship:
      a) so they can receive grants (*GBC Echtemach and A Moritz v Netherlands Minister for Education 389/87 and 390/87*);
      b) and may be exempt from fees if nationals are (*Forcheri v Belgian State 152/82*).

9.7 THE RIGHT TO REMAIN AFTER EMPLOYMENT

1. In Regulation 1251/70 implementing A39(3)(d) 'right of residence acquired by workers in active employment has as a corollary right to remain after having been employed … such rights shall be extended to family; and in case of death of worker during his working life, maintenance of right of residence of members of family must also be recognised …'.

2. A2(1) gives the right to remain permanently to retired workers, incapacitated workers, frontier workers.
3. A3 gives family the right to remain permanently:
   - if the worker is entitled to remain; or
   - if the worker dies during working life and:
     (i) two years' continuous residence in member state;
     (ii) died from occupational disease/accident at work;
     (iii) surviving spouse is a national of the state or lost such nationality by marriage to the worker.
4. The same provisions apply on, for example, residence permits, equal treatment, social advantage, etc.

9.8 FREE MOVEMENT AND PROFESSIONAL SPORT

1. Sport, particularly football, raises problems under A39, i.e. transfer system, limitations on numbers of foreign players.
2. The ability of managers to move freely throughout the community has been established (*Unectef v Heylens 222/86*).
3. The ECJ in the Bosman ruling has major implications for football:
   - A39 prohibits transfer fees once a contract has terminated;
   - it restricts numbers (*Bosman C-415/93*).

9.9 SOCIAL SECURITY PROVISIONS

1. A42 requires aggregation of all periods of work in the community for eligibility to benefits.
2. Implemented by Regulation 1408/71 – does not harmonise social security systems but requires application of systems so as not to penalise worker and prevent him using A39.
3. The key principles are:
   - universality of eligibility and of benefits;
   - non-discrimination (meaning migrant workers cannot be excluded from national systems);
   - aggregated and not concurrent benefits.

9.10 LIMITATIONS ON FREE MOVEMENT

1. Contained in A39(3) – member states can introduce rules which limit the exercise of free movement based 'on grounds of public policy, public security or public health …'.
2. Directive 64/221 lays down principles on all three – extends to all Community nationals who reside in or travel in another member state, as employees, self-employed, or as families.
3. A2 – derogation cannot be used for economic ends.
4. By A3, measures taken on public policy or public security:
   - must be taken exclusively on the conduct of the individual concerned (*Van Duyn v The Home Office 41/74*);
   - and personal conduct is strictly interpreted (*Rutili v Ministere de l'Interieure 36/75*).
5. Public policy can only be invoked where there is a genuine threat to the interests of society (*R v Bouchereau 30/77*). Also:
   - past convictions alone are insufficient to invoke the exception (*Bonsignore v Oberstadtdirecktor of the City of Cologne 67/74*);
   - exclusion cannot be for activity not illegal in the host state (*Adoui and Cornaille v Belgian State 115/81 and 116/81*);
   - mere expiry of an ID card or passport is never sufficient ground for deportation (*Watson and Bellman 118/75*).
6. The difference between public policy and public security is vague.
7. A4 identifies prescribed diseases justifying refusal of entry:
   - any disease endangering public health, e.g. syphilis, TB;
   - drug addiction and profound mental disturbances can justify deportation or refusal of entry.
8. Procedural safeguards include:
   - A5 – decision to refuse entry must be taken within six months, during which time person is allowed to stay;
   - A6 – must give a reason for refusing entry, except if the reason involves national security (*Rutili*);
   - must have the same rights of appeal and remedies as national in respect of administrative decisions;

- if no right of appeal then the individual must have had right of appeal to a court of law of competent authority.

9.11 PUBLIC SERVICE EMPLOYMENT

1. A39(4) allows member states to deny/restrict access to workers in public service on the basis of their nationality.
2. But the ECJ has interpreted this provision fairly narrowly:
   - it does not apply to all public service, only exercise of civil authority or security of state (*Commission v Belgium (Re Public Employees) 149/79*);
   - it applies only to access to employment not to conditions (*Sotgiu v Deutsche Bundespost 152/73*);
   - so cannot reserve posts in hospitals for nationals (*Commission v France (Re French Nurses) 307/84*);
   - or in teaching (*Bleis v Ministere de l'Education C-4/91*);
   - or impose unnecessary qualifications on non-nationals (*Groener Minister for Education 397/87*).

CHAPTER 10

A43 AND FREEDOM OF ESTABLISHMENT, A49 AND THE RIGHT TO PROVIDE SERVICES

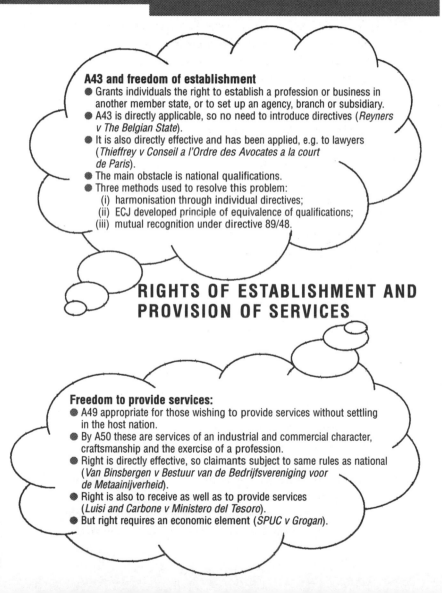

A43 and freedom of establishment
- Grants individuals the right to establish a profession or business in another member state, or to set up an agency, branch or subsidiary.
- A43 is directly applicable, so no need to introduce directives (*Reyners v The Belgian State*).
- It is also directly effective and has been applied, e.g. to lawyers (*Thieffrey v Conseil a l'Ordre des Avocates a la court de Paris*).
- The main obstacle is national qualifications.
- Three methods used to resolve this problem:
   (i) harmonisation through individual directives;
   (ii) ECJ developed principle of equivalence of qualifications;
   (iii) mutual recognition under directive 89/48.

RIGHTS OF ESTABLISHMENT AND PROVISION OF SERVICES

Freedom to provide services:
- A49 appropriate for those wishing to provide services without settling in the host nation.
- By A50 these are services of an industrial and commercial character, craftsmanship and the exercise of a profession.
- Right is directly effective, so claimants subject to same rules as national (*Van Binsbergen v Bestuur van de Bedrijfsvereniging voor de Metaainijverheid*).
- Right is also to receive as well as to provide services (*Luisi and Carbone v Ministero del Tesoro*).
- But right requires an economic element (*SPUC v Grogan*).

10.1 INTRODUCTION

1. Both rights were essential to the creation of a single market.
2. The right to establish is contained in Articles 43–48:
   - It refers to the right of free movement of both the self-employed and professionals.
   - It can include 'legal' as well as natural persons.
   - It is the right to set up and carry out a business, trade or profession in another member state.
3. The freedom to provide services is in Articles 49, 50 and 55. It complements the right of establishment by allowing a person established in one state to exercise a business or profession in another state, so is a temporary right not linked to residence.
4. There is an obvious overlap between the two principles, and some similarity with A39 – and both are subject to the same derogations in directive 64/221.
5. In either case the requirement is that the person should be subject to the same condition as nationals.
6. The major barrier to the freedoms is national qualifications or requirements.

10.2 FREEDOM OF ESTABLISHMENT

1. A43 provides that 'restrictions on the freedom of establishment of nationals of one member state in the territory of another shall be abolished ... such progressive abolition shall also apply to restrictions on the setting up of agencies, branches or subsidiaries ...'.
   - A44 calls for a 'general programme for the abolition of existing restrictions'.
   - By A47 directives will 'make it easier for persons to take up and pursue activities as self-employed ...'.
   - A48 extends provisions to setting up and managing undertakings, particularly companies and firms.

2. A43 is directly applicable, so introducing directives is not vital (*Reyners v The Belgian State 2/74*).
3. It is also directly effective, so can be applied in a variety of circumstances:
   - *Thieffrey v Conseil a l'Ordre des Avocates a la cour de Paris 71/76* and lawyers;
   - *Patrick v Ministre des Affaires Culturelles 11/77* and architects;
   - *Van Ameyde v Ufficio Centrale Italiano di Assistenza Assiscurativa Automobilisti in Circolazione Internazionale 90/76* and a motor insurance claims investigator.
4. The main barrier to the freedoms is national regulation of trades and professions based on national qualifications.
5. Three methods have been devised to resolve this problem:
   - harmonisation of professional qualifications;
   - 'equivalence' of qualifications using the principle of non-discrimination;
   - 'mutual recognition' of qualifications by directive 89/48.
6. Harmonisation is achieved only by a complex, time consuming process of introducing individual directives for individual trades, e.g.:
   - retail trade and Directive 68/363;
   - doctors and Directive 93/16;
   - architects and Directive 85/384;
   - lawyers and Directive 77/249 (but only limited rights to practice).

   The effect is that a person qualified in one state may then practice in another.
7. Equivalence was developed because harmonisation was a slow process and impossible in certain activities. So the ECJ devised the principle that, while member states could still regulate on qualifications, a person having equivalent qualifications has a right to have them taken into account:
   - any refusal to do so must be reasoned and based on insufficiency;
   - the person must be allowed to do further training to make

up the deficiency (*Thieffrey v Conseil de l'Ordre des Avocates a la cour de Paris 71/76*);

- and A43 can be used to challenge any discriminatory practice preventing the pursuit of an activity (*Steinhauser v City of Biarritz 197/84*).

8. Directive 89/48 introduced a general system for mutual recognition of 'higher education diplomas':
   - These are qualifications taking three years or more.
   - The directive applies if no harmonising directive exists.
   - This means that member states must recognise the qualifications of other states so that a person can establish without needing to re-qualify.
   - However, a substantial difference can lead to requirement of an aptitude test or an adaptation period.

10.3 THE FREEDOM TO PROVIDE SERVICES

1. A49 provides for the abolition of restrictions on the freedom to provide services by non-nationals who are not established in the state of the recipient. So is designed for those wishing to provide services without settling in the host nation.
2. Services are identified in Article 50(1) as those normally provided for remuneration, not related to free movement of capital, goods or workers, 'of an industrial and commercial character, craftsmanship and the exercise of a profession ...'
3. The right is directly effective:
   - so claimants are subject to the same rules of professional conduct as nationals (*Van Binsbergen v Bestuur van de Bedrijfsvereniging voor de Metaalnijverheid 33/74*);
   - but the right can only be denied where there is an imperative reason of public interest.
4. The important corollary of the rule is the enforceable freedom to receive services (*Luisi and Carbone v Ministero del Tesoro 286/82*):
   - this principle has been extended to cover access to

education and vocational training (*Gravier v City of Liege 293/83*);
- so vocational courses must be offered on equal terms to all EC citizens (*Blaizot v University of Liege 24/86*);
- but state, secondary education is not a service (*Belgium v Humbel 263/86*);
- and maintenance grants are outside of the scope of the article (*Brown v Secretary of State for Scotland 197/86*).

5. The principle of non-discrimination has been extended out further to include receipt of state compensation (*Cowan v French Treasury 186/87*).

6. However, this is unavailable without an economic element (*SPUC v Grogan C-159/80*).

10.4 RESIDENCE RIGHTS

1. Directive 90/364 grants rights of residence to non-workers who are unable to gain residence under any other provision of EC law.

2. The right is to be treated the same as nationals:
   - It is extended to families and dependants in the same way as A39.
   - But it depends on the person having sufficient resources to avoid becoming a burden on the state.

3. Directive 90/366 extended rights of residence to students enrolled in recognised vocational training which includes rights of spouses, etc. This has now been replaced by Directive 93/96

4. The same derogations as for free movement of workers apply.

5. For freedom of establishment and to provide services generally there is no equivalent to regulation 1612/68, so instead the ECJ used, for example, A12 to gain rights.

CHAPTER 11

EC COMPETITION LAW

11.1 THE PURPOSE AND CHARACTER OF COMPETITION LAW

11.1.1 The purpose of competition law

1. A2 sees the task of EC law as 'the promotion of harmonious development of economic activities by the creation of a common market and the progressive approximation of the economic policies of the member states…'.

2. A3(g) states that the EC must ensure that 'competition in the internal market is not distorted…'.

3. So, the framers of the Treaty:
   - recognised that unfettered market forces can lead directly to anti-competitive practices;
   - inserted rules to deal with this based on the Sherman Act model.

4. These rules had three principal objectives:
   - to avoid restrictive practices and agreements (A81);
   - to prevent large businesses from abusing their market dominance (A82);
   - to apply similar rules to the public sector (A86).

5. EC competition law is criticised because:
   - all practices are treated alike, even if they would benefit the consumer;
   - policy has been said to sacrifice equity and efficiency to political goals;
   - Ian Ward says its existence is 'a perversity' and 'the loud admission of defeat' and 'an admission that the market alone cannot effect competition';
   - there is always the danger of member states clinging to national interests.

6. But the EC has succeeded in framing cohesive and consistent objectives, identified in the Commission's Ninth Report on Competition Policy:
   - creation of an open and unified market not partitioned by restrictive and anti-competitive agreements;
   - realisation of effective competition avoiding over-concentration or abuses by dominant companies;
   - achieving fairness in the market place, giving support to small and medium sized firms, protecting the consumer, and penalising unlawful state subsidies;
   - maintaining the competitive position of the EU against rivals in global economy.

11.1.2 The character of competition law

1. It covers everything – goods, services and intellectual property rights.
2. Provisions are framed in broad terms, so are subject to ECJ interpretation.
3. It can be used against firms regardless of existence of registered office in the EU.
4. Rules are pragmatic, so are subject to exceptions to preserve market efficiency.
5. Penalties apply where trade in the EU is affected, so can apply to small firms and inter-state disputes
6. So, it is possible for EC law and national law to co-exist (*Wilhelm v Bundeskartellamt 23/67*).
7. A81 and A82 are complimentary, pursuing the same objectives by focusing on different types of activity.

The basic A81 prohibition:

- Rule prohibits 'agreements between undertakings, decisions of associations of undertakings and concerted practices which may affect trade between member states having as object prevetion, restriction or distortion of competition within common market'.
- Undertakings defined by ECJ as 'single organisation of personal, tangible and intangible elements, attached to an autonomous legal entity and pursuing a long term economic aim' (*Mannesmann v High Authority*), e.g. a trade association (*FRUGO v Commission*).
- Commission can grant exemption or negative clearance.

A81 AND RESTRICTIVE PRACTICES

Activities beyond scope of A81:

Negative clearance:
- by application to Commission if unsure (or comfort letter).

De minimis rule:
- if less than 5% market share;
- turnover under 200 million ECU.

Commercial agents and subsidiaries.

Exemptions if:
- contributes to improving production or distribution of goods or promoting technical or economic progress (*Transocean Marine Paint Association*);
- consumer gets fair share of benefit (*ACEC v Berliet*);
- no unnecessary restrictions (*Consten and Grundig v Commission*);
- no risk of eliminating competition (*Re Fine Papers*);
- can be individual or block.

Elements proving breach of A81:

Agreements between undertakings, decisions by associations of undertakings, concerted practices:
- must involve collusive behaviour (*AEG Telefunken v Commission*);
- decisions by undertakings are usually by trade associations on, e.g. fixing discounts, collective boycotts, restrictive contract clauses;
- concerted practices are a form of co-ordination between enterprises that has not yet reached the point where it is a contract (*ICI Ltd v Commission (The Dyestuffs Case)*);
- A81 identifies some prohibited arrangements, e.g.:
  - (i) price fixing (*VBVB and VVVB v Comission*);
  - (ii) limiting production (*The Quinine Cartel case*);
  - (iii) sharing markets or suppliers (*Siemens/Franc*);
  - (iv) applying dissimilar conditions to equivalent transactions (*IZA International Belgium*).

Affecting trade between member states:
- ascertained by reference to free movement and attainment of single market;
- must be capable of constituting a threat, direct or indirect, actual or potential, on the pattern of trade (*Belasco v Commission*);
- no need to prove harm, just that agreement may prevent, restrict or distort competition sufficiently (*Vereniging van Cementhandelaren v Commission*).

Object or effect of preventing, restricting or distorting competition:
- as much to do with practical outcomes as intentions;
- key issue is whether or not competition is affected (*Consten and Grundig v Commission*);
- ECJ try to apply the rules so as not to stifle enterprise and initiative (*Societe Technique Miniere v Maschinenbau Ulm*).

11.2 A81 AND RESTRICTIVE PRACTICES

11.2.1 The basic prohibition in A81

1. By A81, 'All agreements between undertakings, decisions of associations of undertakings and concerted practices which may affect trade between member states and which have as their object or effect the prevention, restriction or distortion of competition within the common market' are prohibited.
2. A81 also gives particular examples of anti-competitive acts – those which:
   - directly or indirectly fix purchase or selling prices or any other trading conditions;
   - limit or control production, markets, technical development, or investment;
   - share markets or sources of supply;
   - apply dissimilar conditions to equivalent transactions with other trading parties, thereby placing them at a competitive disadvantage;
   - make the conclusion of contracts subject to acceptance by the other parties of supplementary obligations which, by their nature, have no connection with the subject of such contracts.
3. A81(2) makes all such agreements void, but by A81(3) the Commission can grant exemptions, and 'negative clearance' declares the agreement is not in breach of A81.
4. Both A81 and A82 concern conduct of 'undertakings'.
   - The term is not defined in the Treaty, but is given a broad definition by the ECJ: 'a single organisation of personal, tangible and intangible elements, attached to an autonomous legal entity and pursuing a long term economic aim...' (*Mannesmann v High Authority 1962*)).
   - It can therefore cover everything from an individual to a multi-national corporation.

- It has included, for example:
  - (i) an opera singer (*Re Unitel 78/516*);
  - (ii) a sports federation (*Re World Cup 1990 Package Tours 92/521*);
  - (iii) a state-owned corporation (*Italian State v Sacchi 155/73*);
  - (iv) a public agency (*Hofner v Macroton C-41/90*);
  - (v) a trade association (*FRUGO v Commission 71/74*).

11.2.2 The elements of proof for an action under A81

Agreements between undertakings, decisions by associations of undertakings, concerted practices

1. Agreements: always involve some sort of collusive behaviour as distinct from unilateral acts (*AEG Telefunken v Commission 107/82*):
   - can include informal, oral agreements (*Tepea 28/77*);
   - and the so-called 'gentleman's agreements' (*ACF Chemiefarma v Commission 41,44,45/69 (The Quinine Cartel Case)*).
2. Decisions by associations:
   - usually involve rules of trade associations;
   - and prohibited decisions would include: recommending prices, fixing discounts, collective boycotts, restrictive contract clauses;
   - and even non-binding recommendations (*Vereniging van Cementhandelaren v Commission 8/72*).
3. Concerted practices have been defined by the ECJ as: 'a form of co-ordination between enterprises that has not yet reached the point where it is a contract in the true sense of the word, but which, in practice, consciously substitutes co-operation for the risks of competition ...' (*ICI Ltd v Commission 48/69 (The Dyestuffs Case)*).
4. The test is where parallel behaviour is co-operative, so lacks independence (*Cooperatieve Vereeniging 'Suiker Unie' v Commission 40-48,50,54-56,111,113,114/73 (The Sugar Cartel Case)*).

5. Agreements may be:
- horizontal, i.e. between competitors, and may, for example, divide up markets (*The Dyestuffs Case*); or
- vertical, i.e. between undertakings at different levels in the process, and may be, for example, exclusive distribution arrangements, or licensing agreements.

6. The Article identifies specific prohibited arrangements:
- Price fixing, which may be agreements on, for example, discounts, credit, etc., and have included:
  - (i) agreements between zinc producers (*Re Zinc Producers Group*);
  - (ii) agreements between Italian glass manufacturers (*Re Italian Flat Glass Cartel*);
  - (iii) a retail price maintenance agreement between Belgian and Dutch booksellers (*VBVB and VVVB v Commission 43 and 63/82*).
- Limiting production, where undertakings restrict their own growth to artificially raise prices and prevent outsiders entering the agreement (*The Quinine Cartel case*).
- Sharing markets or sources of supply:
  - (i) can involve carving up markets (either geographically or by product);
  - (ii) and is common in oligopolies where competitors give each other exclusive dealerships (*Siemens/Franc 1985*).
- Applying dissimilar conditions to equivalent transactions:
  - (i) to place another party at a disadvantage;
  - (ii) so might involve giving advantageous conditions to another party (*IZA International Belgium 96–102, 104, 105, 108, 110/82*).
- Imposing supplementary obligations: those with no relationship with actual subject of contract.

Affecting trade between member states

1. In order to breach A81 the agreement must affect trade between member states.

2. This is ascertained by reference to the free movement of goods and attainment of a single market.

3. So it must be capable of constituting a threat 'direct or indirect, actual or potential, on the pattern of trade...' (*Belasco v Commission 246/86*).

4. So there is no need to prove actual harm as long as the agreement is likely to prevent, restrict or distort competition to a sufficient degree (*Vereniging van Cementhandelaren v Commission 8/72*).

The object or effect of preventing, restricting or distorting competition

1. 'Object' and 'effect' are clearly meant to be alternatives, so the test is as much to do with practical outcomes as intentions

2. So, the key issue is whether competition has been affected, not whether trade has gone up or down (*Consten and Grundig v Commission 56 and 58/64*).

3. The ECJ tries to apply the rules so as not to stifle enterprise and initiative (*Societe Technique Miniere v Maschinenbau Ulm 56/65*).

4. It will also apply the *de minimis* rule (*Frans Volk v Establissments Vervaecke Sprl 5/69*).

11.2.3 Activities falling outside of the scope of A81

1. Negative clearance:
   - Undertakings seek negative clearance when they are unsure whether an agreement may violate A81.
   - Undertakings to the Commission by 'notification' seeking clarification that practice is excluded from EC law.
   - If so, certification to this effect is made in a decision.
   - It is an expensive process, so sometimes undertakings seek only a 'comfort letter', which does not give complete protection.

2. 1997 *de minimis* notice – agreements not caught by A81 if less than a 5% market share for the goods or services in the

area of the common market covered by the agreement if horizontal, or 10% if vertical – though a blacklist exists of agreements not tolerated whatever the level of effect.

3. Commercial relations to which the rules do not apply:
   - commercial agents, where they are simply concerned with negotiating transactions for the principal, and assume no financial risk;
   - subsidiaries and parent companies, as the subsidiary has no autonomous decision making capacity (but may breach A82).

4. Exemptions:
   - A81(3) creates criteria for exempting agreements.
   - There are four conditions (two positive, two negative) to be met before exemption is granted:
     (i) the agreement, decision or practice must contribute to improving production or distribution of goods or promoting technical or economic progress (*Transocean Marine Paint Association (D1967) and Re Vacuum Interrupters (No 1)* (D1977));
     (ii) A fair share of the resulting benefit must accrue to the consumer, which is not merely the end consumer (*ACEC v Berliet* (D1968));
     (iii) no unnecessary restrictions should be imposed, e.g. absolute territorial protections (*Consten and Grundig v Commission*);
     (iv) there must be no possibility of the restrictions eliminating competition in respect of a substantial part of the product in question (*Re Fine Papers* (D1972)).
   - Individual exemptions.
     (i) granted under procedure in Regulation 17/62;
     (ii) the application is by 'notification' to the Commission and granted in the form of decisions;
     (iii) it may be for limited periods and depend on fulfilling certain criteria.

- Block exemptions:
  - (i) introduced to reduce the bureaucratic burden of applications for individual exemptions;
  - (ii) granted in Regulations covering specific types of agreements;
  - (iii) Examples include:
    - exclusive distribution 1983/83;
    - exclusive purchasing 1984/83;
    - patent licensing 2349/84;
    - motor vehicle distribution 123/85;
    - know-how licensing 556/89;
    - Regulation 2790/99 (in force June 2000) exempts all vertical agreements except certain serious restraints.

5. Comfort letters – issued but not legally binding.

The basic prohibition:
- A82 involves the concentration of economic power in an undertaking.
- Any abuse of commercial dominance is prohibited if it would affect trade between member states.
- A82 can also apply to oligopolies (*The Flat Glass case*).
- Negative clearance and exemptions are not available (except for mergers).
- Three requirements:
  - (i) dominant position in market;
  - (ii) abuse of dominant position;
  - (iii) affects trade between member states.

A82 ABUSE OF A DOMINANT POSITION

The abuse:
- Defined in case law as behaviour which influences structure of market so that competition is weakened, and maintenance or growth of competition is hindered.
- So could include, e.g.
  - differential pricing for different member states (*United Brands*);
  - 'tying arrangements' (*Tetra Pak II*);
  - dissimilar conditions;
  - limiting markets, technical development, production (*Magill TV Guide & ITP v Commission*).

Affecting inter-state trade:
- must result from the abuse.

Existence of dominance:
- Dominance defined in ECSC Treaty – undertaking holds position shielding it against effective competition.
- The ECJ has also defined dominance and 'the power to control production or distribution for a significant part of the products in question' (*Continental Can Co. v Commission*) and 'a position of economic strength ... which enables it to prevent competition being maintained' (*United Brands*).
- Need to consider:
  - (i) relevant market;
  - (ii) market share.
- Relevant product market decided on whether there is sufficient interchangeability between all the products forming part of the same market (*Hoffman-la-Roche v Commission*).
- So could be, e.g. separate cartons for pasteurised and UHT milk (*Tetra Pak (No 1)*).
- Geographical market should be whole community, but can take into account other factors, e.g. costs and feasibility of transport (*Hilti v Commission*).
- Temporal market may involve, e.g. seasonal factors (*United Brands*).
- No particular market share needed for dominance, e.g. 40% share in *United Brands* insufficient.
- Should consider, e.g.:
  - (i) market share *Hoffman-la-Roche*);
  - (ii) competitor's share (*United Brands*).

11.3 A82 AND ABUSE OF A DOMINANT POSITION

11.3.1 Introduction

1. A81 concerns collusion between undertakings, but A82 usually concerns actions of a single undertaking.
2. So, the threat to competition is the concentration of economic power.
3. By A82, 'Any abuse by one or more undertakings of a dominant position within the common market or in a substantial part of it shall be prohibited as incompatible with the common market insofar as it may affect trade between member states':
   - specific examples of abuses are identified;
   - A81 and A82 are not mutually exclusive, so there is discretion which to claim under;
   - A82 can apply also to oligopolies (*The Flat Glass Case* (D1989)).
4. A82 also deals with mergers and concentrations.
5. There are overlaps with A81 – negative clearance and exemptions are not available (though they are for mergers).
6. A82 does not prohibit dominant positions, only abuses, so is not meant to punish efficient economic behaviour.
7. There are three requirements that must be shown:
   - that the undertaking has a dominant position in the market;
   - that the practice in question abuses that dominant position;
   - that trade between member states is affected as a result.

11.3.2 The existence of a dominant position

1. Dominance is not defined in the Treaty, but it is in the ECSC Treaty where undertakings hold a position 'shielding them against effective competition in a substantial part of the common market ...'.

2. So it is left to the ECJ, as usual, to define in the cases:
- 'power to behave independently without taking into account their competitors, purchasers or suppliers because of their share of the market or ... availability of technical knowledge, raw materials or capital, they have power to control production or distribution for significant part of products' (*Continental Can Co. v Commission 6/72*);
- 'a position of economic strength ... which enables it to prevent competition being maintained on the relevant market by giving it the power to behave to an appreciable effect independently of its competitors, and ultimately its consumers' (*United Brands v Commission 27/76*);
- 'such a position does not preclude some competition but enables (it) ... if not to determine, at least to have an appreciable effect on the conditions in which that competition will develop, and in any case to act largely in disregard of it' (*Hoffman-la-Roche v Commission 85/76*).

3. So there are two key concepts in determining dominance:
- relevant product market and geographical market;
- calculation of market share.

The relevant product market

1. Dominant undertakings will want the product market defined broadly; those affected for it to be defined narrowly.

2. So, product market includes the product plus all products which may be perfectly substituted for it.
- It is measured on whether there is 'sufficient interchangeability between all products forming part of same market insofar as specific use of products is concerned ...' (*Hoffman-la-Roche v Commission*).
- The relevant market depends on 'cross elasticity of demand' and 'supply'.

3. Examples of the relevant market have included:
- heavy goods vehicle tyres as opposed to tyres generally (*Michelin (NV Nederlandsche Baden-Indutrie Michelin) v Commission 322/81*);

- cash register parts (*Hugin Kassaregister AB v Commission 22/78*);
- separate cartons for pasteurised and UHT milk (*Tetra Pak (No 1) T-51/89*).

Geographical market

1. This is 'where the conditions of competition are sufficiently homogenous for the effect of economic power on the undertaking to be evaluated ...' (*United Brands*).
2. In general, the relevant market must be the whole Community, but situations of producers in busy commercial areas are different to those in remote rural areas, even if they enjoy the same market share.
3. So other things will inevitably be taken into account:
   - cost, feasibility of transport (*Hilti v Commission T-30/89*);
   - pattern/volume of consumption (*Suiker Unie 40/73*).

Temporal market

1. Seasonal factors may be relevant if there is no substitution (*United Brands*).

Calculation of market share

1. No particular market share is required to prove dominance, e.g. a 40% share in *United Brands* was not sufficient on its own – other factors were relevant, e.g. owned own fleet, could control volume of other imports, and highly fragmented rest of market.
2. So other factors must be considered, e.g.:
   - competitors' market share was 10% and 16% in *United Brands*;
   - superior technological knowledge and sales network in *Michelin*;
   - control of production/distribution in *Hoffman-la-Roche*;
   - conduct/performance.

11.3.3 The abuse of the dominant position

1. The abuse, not existence, of dominant position is prohibited.
2. There is no definition of abuse in the Article – though there are some examples.
3. So, again it is defined by the ECJ: 'behaviour ... which is such as to influence the structure of the market where, as a result of the very presence of the undertaking in question, the degree of competition is weakened, and ... has the effect of hindering the maintenance of the degree of competition ... or the growth of that competition ...'.
4. Specific practices identified as abuses in the Article include:
   - directly or indirectly imposing unfair purchase or selling prices or other unfair trading conditions, e.g.:
       (i) price reduction to kill competition (*AKZO v Commission C-62/86*);
       (ii) differential pricing for different states (*United Brands*);
       (iii) loyalty rebates (*Hoffman-la-Roche*);
   - limiting production, markets or technical development to the prejudice of consumers (*Magill TV Guide and ITP v Commission C-241/91 P*);
   - applying dissimilar conditions to equivalent transactions with other trading parties, thereby placing them at a competitive disadvantage;
   - making conclusion of contracts subject to supplementary obligations having no connection with subject of such contracts, e.g. 'tying arrangements' (*Tetra Pak II* (1992)).

11.3.4 Affecting trade between member states

1. This must be an effect caused by the abuse.
2. The same condition is imposed in A81.
3. It is not hard to show.

11.4 MERGER CONTROL

11.4.1 Merger control under A81 and A82

1. Prior to 1990 only standard competition law was available to deal with mergers and concentrations.
2. Both needed control because the nature of monopoly power is anti-competitive.
3. So, A82 might be infringed if a dominant undertaking strengthened its dominance so that the only undertakings to remain in the relevant market are those whose behaviour depends on the dominant one (*Europembellage Corporation and Continental Can v Commission 6/72*).

11.4.2 Merger control under Regulation 4064/89

1. Pressure for effective legislation grew by late 1980s.
2. It came in Regulation 4064/89.
3. The purpose of the Regulation is to identify mergers of such a size that they should be controlled by the EC rather than by national authorities.
4. So, the Regulation concerns 'concentrations': 'significant changes in ownership over companies which could distort competition …'.
5. 'Concentrations' meeting certain criteria must be 'notified' to the Commission within one week of the agreement being concluded, if they have a Community dimension:
   ● the undertakings concerned must have a combined world turnover of at least 5,000 million ECUs; and
   ● the total Community-wide turnover of at least two of the undertakings must be exceed 250 million ECUs;
   ● but there will be no Community dimension and so no infringement where each of the parties does not derive two-thirds of its business in the EC in a single member state.

11.4.3 Procedure

1. The test for the Commission is whether the concentration creates or enhances a dominant position that would lead to effective competition being substantially impeded.

2. Once notified the Commission must take one of three decisions:

- decide that the concentration falls within the scope of the Regulation and gives rise to proceedings because it is potentially incompatible with the requirements of a common market;
- decide that it falls within the scope of the Regulation but there is no need for proceedings because it is compatible with common market;
- decide that it falls outside the scope of the Regulation.

3. If proceedings are initiated then the resulting decision must be within four months:

- the Commission can declare the concentration compatible, or if not it can be rescinded;
- the Commission can also fine undertakings which fail to notify a merger.

11.5 PROCEDURAL RULES

11.5.1 Introduction

1. Powers and procedures are found in Regulation 17/62.

2. Subsequently amended but the same mechanisms remain.

3. The fundamental rule is that infringements of A81 and A82 are prohibited regardless of any previous rules.

11.5.2 Range of available options

1. The Commission has wide powers to deal with actual and potential infringements of competition law.

2. It may deal with them in a variety of ways:

- it may give negative clearance (A81);

- it may grant individual exemptions;
- it may make investigations and conclude that there are no grounds to impose a penalty;
- but it will usually try to reach an informal conclusion first, e.g. the issuing of comfort letters.

11.5.3 Notification of agreements

1. All new agreements must be notified to the Commission.
2. The Commission may then prevent imposition of fines, but will not prevent an agreement which is an infringement from being invalidated.
3. Notification is on prescribed forms.

11.5.4 The investigative power of the Commission

1. The Commission can instigate an investigation:
   - either on its own initiative; or
   - on application of member state or interested parties;
   - it may only take action after an 'appropriate preliminary investigation';
   - and if it decides to act it must notify the applicants.
2. It has extensive power to obtain information from governments, relevant authorities, firms, etc., so it has the right to:
   - examine books and other business records;
   - take copies or extracts from any of these;
   - request on-the-spot oral explanations;
   - enter any premises or transport of the undertaking.

11.5.5 Judicial powers of the Commission

1. Undertakings must be allowed a fair hearing.
2. The Commission arranges hearings, having circulated a 'Statement of Objections' – all parties can respond.
3. The hearing is then within two months.

11.5.6 Available penalties

1. The Commission can impose two types of financial penalty:
- Fines: from 1,000–1,000,000 ECUs, or a larger amount not over 10% of annual global turnover. The amount depends on seriousness and duration of infringement, subject to 1998 Notice on method of setting fines.
- Periodic payments: incentive led penalties. The penalty is a specific sum for every day or week the infringement continues, so is an incentive to stop quickly. Payments can vary between 50 and 1,000 ECUs

11.5.7 Review by the Court of First Instance

1. By 17/62 Commission decisions are reviewable by court.
2. They will take the form of A230 or A232 actions.

11.5.8 Enforcement by national authorities

1. Enforcement of competition law would be impossible without the assistance of national authorities, so they can be involved in various ways.
2. They may initiate the investigation by application to the Commission.
3. Under A13 they may make their own investigations, and may do so at the request of the Commission.
4. Domestic courts may also apply A81 and A82, but only where the Commission is not already involved, because A81 and A82 are both directly effective (*BRT v Sabam 127/73*).
5. However, national courts cannot issue exemptions (only the Commission can), but they can award damages for parties affected by infringements, and also grant injunctive relief.

CHAPTER 12

A141 AND ANTI-DISCRIMINATION LAW

Equal pay:
- By A141 'men and women shall receive equal pay for equal work'.
- A141 is directly effective (*Defrenne v SABENA*).
- Comparitor need not be in contemporaneous empoyment (*Macarthys v Smith*).
- Wide definition of pay – ordinary basic or minimum wage or salary or any other consideration, whether in cash or in kind, received directly or indirectly – so could include concessionary travel (*Garland v BREL*) and contracted out pension (*Barber v Guardian Royal Assurance Group*) etc.
- Supplemented and explained in directive 75/117, which includes an action for work of equal value (*Hayward v Camel Laird Shipbuilders*).
- But can only receive equal pay, even if work shown to be of superior value (*Murphy v An Bord Telecom Eireann*).
- Possible to pay differential pay rates to part-timers provided there is an 'objective justification' (*Bilka-Kaufhaus*) if:
    (i) corresponds to genuine need of enterprise;
    (ii) suitable for obtaining objective pursued by the enterprise;
    (iii) necessary for that purpose.

Equal access:
- Found in directive 76/207 – in access to employment, including promotion and to vocational training and … working conditions there shall be equal treatment for men and women.
- Derogation permitted for activities where sex is a dermining factor (*Johnston v RUC*) or for protection of women.
- But positive discrimination not allowed (*Kalanke v Frei Hausestadt Bremen*).
- Has beeen used in pregnancy on dismissl (*Webb v EMO (Air Cargo)*) or employment denied (*Dekker v Stichting*).
- Has been used for unequal retirement ages (*Marshall v Southampton AHA*).
- Usual problems associated with direct effect of directives, but may be indirectly effective under the *Von Colson* principle (*Beets-Proper v F. Van Lanschot Bankiers NV*).

DISCRIMINATION LAW

Social security:
- Directive 79/7 extends equal access principle to social security.
- Applies to statutory schemes protecting against sickness, invalidity, old age, accidents at work, occupational diseases, and unemployment.
- Can exclude: deciding pensionable age, benefits for people who have brought up children, wives' derived invalidity or old age benefits, increases granted to dependent wife.

Future developments:
- Two directives due to be implemented in 2003 or 2006:
    (i) one on race
    (ii) one more general includes, e.g. sexual orientation.

Self-employment
- Found in directive 86/613.
- Applies to all persons pursuing a gainful activity for their own account.
- Ensures member states eliminate discrimination.

12.1 INTRODUCTION

1. Equality is a fundamental principle of EC law, and is used as one of the general principles of law, so all measures are ultimately subject to it.
2. Sexual equality was seen as a natural extension of the principle of national equality.
3. A141, then, was one of the first substantive provisions created to ensure that two distinct objectives are achieved:
   - an economic objective – the elimination of unfair advantages which would distort free competition;
   - a social objective – the general improvement of living and working conditions throughout the Community.
4. A141 is simply stated and requires that 'member states shall ensure that … men and women receive equal pay for equal work …'.
5. It has since been supplemented by many directives:
   - 75/117 – the Equal Pay Directive;
   - 76/207 – the Equal Treatment Directive;
   - 79/7 – the Equal Treatment in Social Security Directive;
   - 86/378 – the Equal Treatment in Occupational Pension Schemes Directive;
   - 86/613 – Equal Treatment in Self-employment Directive.
6. Case law of the ECJ (with the exception of one aspect of *Defrenne v SABENA*) has been consistent in preventing national interests from subverting the general principle:
   - most of the case law in A234 references has involved rectifying the narrow interpretations by national courts;
   - it has been instrumental in developing the law on, for example, fair treatment of pregnant women and other areas.
7. The Commission has also been active, e.g. developing law on sexual harassment – defined in their Code of Practice.
8. A141 is directly effective (*Defrenne v SABENA (No 2) 43/75*):
   - It is effective horizontally and vertically because it is a Treaty article and satisfies all three elements of the *Reyner* test.

- Unfortunately, national demands by the UK and Ireland led to it being only prospectively directly effective.
9. Subsequently, many of the directives have also been held to be directly effective (but only vertically because Directives fail the *Reyner* test), leading to anomalies and so judicial activism by the ECJ (see *Marshall v Southampton and S.W. Havant AHA* and also *Duke v Reliance GEC*).

12.2 A141 AND EQUAL PAY

1. The ECJ has had none of the problems encountered by, for example, English courts in establishing the existence of a comparitor of the opposite sex (*Macarthys v Smith 129/79*).
2. Most actions in the ECJ have focused on the meaning of pay:
   - defined in A141 as 'the ordinary basic or minimum wage or salary or any other consideration, whether in cash or in kind, which the worker receives directly or indirectly, in respect of his employment from his employer';
   - so pay has a much broader meaning in A141 than in the Equal Pay Act, and interpretation is purposive.
3. Pay has been held to include:
   - perks, e.g. concessionary rail fares for retired railway workers (*Garland v BREL 12/81*) and supplementary payments into an occupational pension scheme (*Worringham and Humphries v Lloyds Bank Ltd 69/80*);
   - sick pay (*Rinner-Kuhn v FWW Spezial Gebaudereinigung GmbH and Co. KG 171/88*);
   - paid leave for training (*Arbeiterwehlifahrt der Stadt Berlin v Botel*);
   - contractual non-contributory occupational pension schemes, supplementing state schemes, denied to part-timers (*Bilka-Kaufhaus v Karen Weber von Harz 170/84*);
   - unequal retirement ages (*Marshall v Southampton and South West Hampshire AHA (Teaching) (No 1) 152/84*);
   - redundancy payments (*R v Secretary of State for Employment ex parte Equal Opportunities Commission (1994) (HL)*);

- EAT has suggested it may include compensation for unfair dismissal (*Mediguard Services Ltd v Thame* (1994));
- 'contracted out' pension schemes which depend for operation on different retirement ages, as in *Barber v Guardian Royal Assurance Group 262/88*. The case is also important in identifying that A141 is infringed if pension rights are deferred in a person made compulsorily redundant to retirement age (if different to person of opposite sex), so applies *Marshall* logic to contracted out schemes, but had prospective direct effect like *Defrenne*.

4. Pension rights are also covered in the subsequent directives, but the ECJ rulings are important to the UK because death and retirement is not covered by English law in the Equal Pay Act.

5. When considering inequality the ECJ will have regard to every different aspect of pay separately and compare on each level (*Handels-og Kontorfunktionaernes Forbund v Dansk Arbejdsgiverforening for Danfoss 109/88*).

6. This contrasts sharply with the original attitude of the English courts to take a 'whole contract' view (*Hayward v Camel Laird Shipbuilders* (1986)).

7. Contrary to the original UK interpretation of the Equal Pay Act, the ECJ has held that the comparitor need not be in contemporaneous employment (*Macarthys v Smith 129/79*) which is now accepted in English law (*Diocese of Hallam Trustees v Connaughten* (1996)).

8. It may be possible to pay differential pay rates to part-timers and justify discrimination provided there is an 'objective justification' (*Bilka-Kaufhaus*), which it will be if it:
   - corresponds to a genuine need of the enterprise;
   - is suitable for obtaining the objective pursued by the enterprise;
   - is necessary for that purpose.

12.3 THE EQUAL PAY DIRECTIVE – 75/117

1. This was introduced to define the exact meaning of equal pay in A141 'for same work or for work to which equal value is attributed, the elimination of all discrimination on grounds of sex with regards to all aspects and conditions of remuneration ...'.

2. So, importantly, also incorporates the claim for equal pay for work of equal value.

3. 'Same work' does not have to be identical nor need it involve contemporaneous employment (*Macarthys v Smith 129/79*).

4. But discrimination only exists where the differential term is based on sex alone (*Jenkins v Kingsgate Clothing Ltd 96/80*).

5. Discrimination might be direct (*Dekker v Stichting Vormingscentrum Voor Jong Volwassenen C-77/88*) or indirect (*Jenkins v Kingsgate Clothing*), e.g. by giving different rates to part-timers.

6. To bring an 'equal value claim' a woman must show that her job, though different to the man's, is equal in the demands made on her in terms of effort, skill, decision making, etc. and thus of equal value to the employer.

   ● Proving a claim will depend on the result of a job evaluation study instigated as a result of the claim.

   ● ECJ guidelines on such schemes are in *Rummler v Dato-Druck GmbH 237/85*. The scheme could be acceptable if:

   (i) the system as a whole precluded discrimination on grounds of sex;

   (ii) the criteria employed were objectively justified, which they would be if:

   a) appropriate to tasks to be carried out; and

   b) correspond with genuine need of undertaking.

   ● *Danfoss* extended the criteria to include flexibility and seniority.

   ● 75/117 requires member states to ensure that provisions of collective agreements, wage scales, wage agreements, or individual contracts of employment contrary to the principle of equality are invalidated.

- It is also the member state's responsibility to ensure that citizens have the means to bring such a claim – so the UK was taken to the ECJ under A226 infringement proceedings in *Commission v UK 61/81* (leading to the Equal Pay (Amendment) Act 1983, the first claim being *Hayward v Camel Laird Shipbuilders* (1986)), as was Luxembourg in *Commission v Luxembourg 58/81.*

- It has since been shown that provisions in UK law in the Employment Protection Consolidation Act 1978 on part-time workers offend EC law (*R v Secretary of State for Employment, ex parte Equal Opportunities Commission* (1994)).

- The old two-year qualifying period for unfair dismissal was also challenged (*R v Secretary of State for Employment, ex parte Seymour-Smith* (1997)).

- One major anomaly of the 'equal value claim' is that the woman can only receive equal pay, even if her work is shown to be of superior value (*Murphy v An Bord Telecom Eireann 157/86*).

- In some situations a claim could be brought under the Directive or A141, in which case the latter is preferable because of direct effect implications.

12.4 THE EQUAL ACCESS DIRECTIVE – 76/207

1. This was introduced under A308 rather than A141: 'If action by the Community ... necessary to attain ... one of the objectives ... and this Treaty has not provided the necessary powers, the Council shall ... take the appropriate measures ...'.

2. By 76/207, 'as regards access to employment, including promotion and to vocational training and ... working conditions and ... conditions referred to in paragraph 2 social security ... there shall be equal treatment for men and women ...'.

3. Equal treatment is defined in A2 of the Directive: 'no discrimination whatsoever on grounds of sex, either directly or indirectly by reference in particular to marital or family status'.

4. Derogation is permitted under A2(2) for 'activities for which the sex of the worker constitutes a determining factor'. (*Johnston v Chief Constable of the Royal Ulster Constabulary 222/84*).
   - It is for national courts to determine how national legislation is interpreted, but:
     (i) derogation can only apply to specific duties, not activities in general;
     (ii) the situation must be periodically reviewed to ensure it is still justified;
     (iii) the principle of proportionality must apply;
   - derogation is also possible under A2(3) for 'provisions concerning the protection of women, particularly as regards pregnancy and maternity ...', but the same provision will not protect men (*Hofman v Barmer Ersatzkasse 184/83*);
   - and by A2(4), for measures giving 'specific advantage to women with a view to improving their ability to compete in the labour market and to pursue a career on an equal footing with men ...', but not to the extent of using quotas (*Kalanke v Frei Hausestadt Bremen C-450/93*);
   - in *Commission v UK 165/82*, the ECJ held that the UK was in breach of the directive by exempting private households and employers of six or fewer employees, but not for denying men access to midwifery.

5. Directive 76/207 can have particular use in pregnancy:
   - where access to employment is denied (*Dekker v Stichting C-177/88*);
   - or on dismissal during maternity leave (*Hertz 179/80*);
   - or for any dismissal purely on the grounds of pregnancy (*Webb v EMO Air Cargo C-2/93*).

6. It can also be useful in relation to unequal retirement ages

(*Marshall* – although retirement ages generally come under Directive 79/7 *Burton v British Railways Board 19/81*).

7. It can be useful in relation to the calculation of pensionable age for redundancy (*Barber v Guardian Royal Exchange C-262/88*).

8. Under A3(2) of the Directive, member states must ensure that:
   - national laws that deny equal treatment are abolished;
   - any terms in collective agreements, contracts of employment or rules of professional bodies that would deny equal treatment are also annulled.

9. Directive 76/207 has the usual problems associated with direct effect of directives, but may be indirectly effective under the *Von Colson* principle (*Beets-Proper v F. Van Lanschot Bankiers NV 262/84*).

12.5 DIRECTIVE 79/7 AND EQUAL TREATMENT IN MATTERS OF SOCIAL SECURITY

1. This extends the basic principle in 76/207 to social security matters:
   - by A2 it applies to the working population: 'self-employed persons, workers and self-employed persons whose activity is interrupted by illness, accident, or involuntary unemployment and persons seeking employment … retired or invalided workers and self-employed persons …';
   - and it has been interpreted broadly (*Drake v Chief Adjudication Officer 150/85* on carers).

2. Under A3 the principles apply to:
   - statutory schemes giving protection against sickness, invalidity, old age, accidents at work, occupational diseases, and unemployment;
   - social assistance in so far as it is intended to supplement or replace the statutory schemes.

3. Under A4 there will be no discrimination in:
   - the scope of the schemes and conditions of access to them;

- obligation to contribute and calculation of contributions;
- calculation of benefits including cover of benefits;
- duration of the benefit.

4. So it can apply, for example, to invalidity payment to part-time workers (*Ruzius-Wilbrink v Bestuur van de Bedrifsvereniging voor Overheidsdiensten 102/88*).

5. A7 allows member states to exclude certain matters:
   - determination of pensionable age;
   - benefits for people who have brought up children;
   - wives' derived invalidity or old age benefits;
   - increases granted to a dependent wife.

6. But some aspects would come under it, e.g. *Marshall, Burton* and it would not apply to, for example, exemption from prescription charges based on differential pensionable age (*R v Secretary of State for Health ex parte Richardson C-137/94*).

12.6 DIRECTIVE 86/378 AND EQUAL TREATMENT IN OCCUPATIONAL PENSION SCHEMES

1. This was issued to supplement 79/7 and extend equal treatment to occupational schemes 'not governed by Directive 79/7 whose purpose is to provide workers with benefits intended to supplement the benefits provided by the statutory schemes or to replace them …'.

2. However, the Directive is probably all but redundant owing to the decision in *Barber*, which allows that such schemes are pay under A141, and thus the preferable action is under A141.

12.7 DIRECTIVE 86/613 AND EQUAL TREATMENT IN SELF-EMPLOYMENT

1. This extends the principle of equal treatment to self-employment.

2. A2 applies to 'all persons pursuing a gainful activity for their own account – including farmers and members of the liberal professions … and spouses not being employees or partners where they habitually participate in activities of self-employed worker and perform same tasks or ancillary tasks …'.

3. So, member states must ensure that all discrimination is eliminated in:
   - establishment, equipment, extension or launching of any business (A4);
   - formation of companies between spouses (A5);
   - access to social security schemes (A6).

12.8 FUTURE DEVELOPMENTS

1. A141 is now a base for introducing directives based on equality.

2. A141 is still limited to sexual equality, but a separate clause A13 allows the Commission to take appropriate action to combat discrimination based on 'sex, racial or ethnic origin, religion or belief, disability, age, or sexual orientation'.

3. So, the Commission has announced two directives:
   - the first is on race discrimination in employment (and limited specific non-employment areas) – due for implementation in July 2003, so amending legislation enacted in the UK;
   - the second applies to employment only on discrimination on age, sexual orientation, disability, religion, belief.

4. More directives and soft law are due in the Social Policy Agenda.

CHAPTER 13

THE SOCIAL DIMENSION

13.1 A17 AND CITIZENSHIP

1. TEU laid the foundation is of citizenship – a logical progression of the move away from the purely economic view of free movement – now in A17.
2. A18–A22 state the individual rights of citizens:
   - to move and reside freely in member states – A18;
   - to vote and stand as a candidate in municipal elections – A19(1);
   - to vote in or stand for European Parliament – A19(2);
   - to receive diplomatic protection or representation in a state where the citizen's own state is not diplomatically represented – A20;
   - to petition the European Parliament or apply to the ombudsman – A21.
3. Those derogations found in the Treaty can be applied.
4. However, complete free movement will only be achieved with removal of all border controls – all member states other than the UK and Eire have already accepted this principle in the Schengen Agreement.
5. Now the Amsterdam Treaty has integrated policy on free movement, asylum, and immigration – a five-year period has been set for implementation, e.g. of removal of all internal border controls.
6. Problems concerning concept of citizenship include:
   - it is symbolic, without real content;
   - the rights and duties involved are not totally clear;
   - it adds little to citizenship of individual states;
   - non-citizens enjoy similar rights in many cases;
   - it misleadingly suggests the concept of a European state which does not yet exist;

- there is still no real enforceability of two of the three 'pillars' of the Union.
7. But the general idea is to promote a sense of connection with the Union as a whole, as well as with member states.

13.2 SOCIAL POLICY

13.2.1 Background

1. There is no direct mention of social policy in the EC Treaty – policies were originally framed in economic terms.
2. But A136–A145 did set out general aims of 'improved working conditions and standard of living' and A130d established the European Social Fund (ESF).
3. It is said that the social dimension has consistently been compromised by the overriding economic interest.
4. There was little progress in social policy before the mid 1980s, though the first 'Social Action Programme' 1974 did set out objectives of full and better employment; better living and working conditions; social dialogue in the workplace.
5. With change of personnel, e.g. Mitterand, Delors, a new 'Social Action Programme' was agreed, stressing the need for a 'balanced Europe' and 'social and economic cohesion'.
6. A118A and A118B were inserted in the Treaty by SEA '86.
7. Followed by 'The Social Dimension of the Internal Market', recommending creation of a Social Charter, accepted by all but rejected out of hand by the UK – resulted in the Social Protocol following Maastricht.
8. ToA was the most important development for social policy, and introduced a new framework, after the UK agreed.

13.2.2 The Social Charter

1. This is implemented through Social Action Programmes.
2. It lays down 13 fundamental principles to achieve:
   - right of free movement for employment;
   - right to fair remuneration;

- right to employment on same terms as nationals;
- right to improved living and working conditions;
- right to social protection in existing national systems, and minimum income for those without employment;
- right to free association and collective bargaining;
- right to vocational training;
- right of men and women to equal treatment in and out of work;
- rights of workers to information, consultation, and to participation;
- right to protection of health and safety at work;
- protection of children and adolescents;
- guaranteed minimum standard of living for the elderly;
- improvements in both social and professional integration for the disabled.

13.2.3 Treaty of Amsterdam and the new framework

1. A new A136 has been inserted, which recognises the Charter and states new objectives: 'promotion of employment, improved living and working conditions, ... proper social protection, dialogue between management and labour, development of human resources with a view to lasting high employment and combating of exclusion ...'.
2. But it is limited by subsidiarity and economic realism.
3. A137, using Qualified Majority Voting is the method chosen to implement objectives, including: improvement of working environment; information and consultation of workers; integration of those excluded from the labour market; equality between men and women.

13.2.4 The European Social Fund

1. The purpose of the fund in A146 is to improve employment opportunities for workers and contribute, thereby, to raising the standard of living.

2. It is administered by the Commission.

3. It was originally used very much to combat youth unemployment, but the overriding principle now is to compliment forms of aid already emanating from national programmes rather than creating entirely new programmes of aid.

4. Education is, in any case, helped mainly through funding systems such as ERASMUS.

13.3 PROTECTION OF WORKERS

1. Apart from free movement and equality there are a number of ways that EC law has sought to protect workers.

2. Commonly these are introduced as directives through the area of health and safety – A136 refers to the promotion and maintenance of improved working conditions.

3. Although the definition of working conditions is deliberately vague, A137–A140 refer specifically to employment rights, health and safety, training, social security.

4. Directive 89/391 introduced general standards on health and safety at work.

5. Directive 93/104 (the Working Time directive) – is a contentious piece of legislation introduced under the old A118a – now found in A137.

- The directive lays down minimum standards in organising working time, and so maximum work periods (48 hours per week) and minimum rest periods (11 hours out of 24, and 48 hours in every seven-day period) – different periods apply to young workers.
- It also lays down standards in relation to things such as night work.
- It also provides for minimum paid holidays – four weeks.
- But it also allows for wide derogations.

6. Directive 77/187 (the Acquired Rights directive) protects workers when the business they work for is transferred.

- Incorporated in the UK as Transfer of Undertakings (Protection of Employment) Regulations (TUPE).

- It basically transfers rights and obligations to the new employer when there is a 'relevant transfer'.
- The directive has subsequently been modified and amended in directive 98/50.

7. Directive 98/59 (the Collective Redundancies directive) applies to those situations where, for example, the whole work force may be made redundant:
   - it provides for proper consultation procedures;
   - and attempts to avoid the redundancy if possible.

8. Directive 80/987 provides state protection for employees of insolvent employers.

13.4 PROTECTION OF CONSUMERS

1. Before SEA there was little reference in Treaties to consumer protection.
2. Those measures that were introduced had as much to do with protecting free competition as anything else.
3. Prior to this time measures were introduced under the old A100 (now A94) aiming for harmonisation, including:
   - the Product Liability directive 85/374:
     - (i) this imposed strict liability on producers for all damage caused by defective products;
     - (ii) 'producer' was defined broadly so as to include anyone in the chain of supply and distribution, including importers.
   - the Misleading Advertising directive 84/450;
   - the Doorstep Selling directive 85/577;
   - the Consumer Credit directive 87/102.
4. SEA, to speed up harmonisation, took to adopting measures under A100a, allowing qualified majority voting.
5. Measures introduced by the old A100a (now A95) were included:
   - the Toy Safety directive 88/378;
   - the Price Indication directive 88/314;
   - the Package Travel directive 90/314;

- the Unfair Terms in Consumer Contracts directive 93/13.
6. Following Maastricht and the TEU, consumer protection is now accepted as a policy of the EU:
   - to be achieved by internal market measures under A95, and specific actions using the co-decision procedure;
   - measures subsequently adopted include the Timeshare directive 94/47, and the Cross-Border Transfer directive 97/5.
7. The Treaty of Amsterdam also made a commitment to consumer protection in A153, which will be by adopting measures under A95, or by adopting measures that support the policies of member states.
8. Current Commission proposals for developing consumer protection include harmonising laws on sale of goods, on guarantees of consumer goods, on provision of services and on e-commerce.

13.5 THE CHARTER OF RIGHTS

1. Protection of human rights is a general principle of EC law that judges in the ECJ use in interpretation.
2. However, despite many examples of the ECJ referring to the European Convention of Human Rights, and while all member states are signatories to European Convention, there is no formal link between the EU and the Convention.
3. The EU has developed its own 'Charter of Fundamental Rights', the first draft being produced in July 2000.
4. It was formally considered by heads of state at the Biarritz summit in October 2000, and formally adopted by the European Council at the Nice summit in December 2000.
5. The rights identified in the Charter very much overlap with Convention rights – the right to life, the right to personal liberty, protection of workers' rights, protection from discrimination, protection of personal data, etc.
6. The preamble to the Charter states that it is intended to 'enhance protection of human rights in light of changes in

society, social progress, and scientific and technical developments.

7. The Charter is not binding, so it is uncertain what affect it will have on EU policy, rulings in the ECJ, on member states, or on the relationship between EU and ECHR.

CHAPTER 14

THE FUTURE

14.1 ENLARGEMENT

1. Enlargement is seen as being of two types:
   - expanding the number of member states;
   - deepening the ties of the existing member states.
2. The Commission has already approved the start of negotiations for entry of six more states – Hungary, Czech Republic, Poland, Slovenia, Estonia and Cyprus – and talks on membership – Slovakia, Latvia, Lithuania, Bulgaria, Romania and Malta.
3. On deeper ties:
   - some states, e.g. France, want deeper ties;
   - some states, e.g. the UK, want expanded membership but looser ties between states;
   - in fact, these two are probably incompatible;
   - a third possibility is a 'two-speed' Europe, with some states proceeding with deeper ties at a faster rate than others – this has actually happened in the past with, for example, the protocols following Maastricht.
4. There is also European Economic Area (EEA) – a looser arrangement between the EU, Norway, Iceland and Liechtenstein.

14.2 THE NICE TREATY

This reached a number of decisions on change, including:
   - extension of qualified majority voting to a broader range of policy areas;
   - changes to the balance of voting in the Council on inclusion of other states;
   - changes to the composition of the Commission in the event of there being more than 20 states, or alternatively

membership reflecting the number of states but with
reorganisation of the Commission for efficiency;
- changes to the ECJ and CFI – either to allow CFI to hear
preliminary rulings or to have boards of appeal
determining outcomes of certain cases before going to
ECJ or CFI;
- limiting the size of Parliament to 700 MEPs, whatever the
number of states in the Union;
- policy of 'enhanced co-operation' (now under ToA) –
allowing certain states to move ahead of others with
certain policies, so decisions are not dependant on the
latter;
- it has been agreed that another IGC should be held in
2004 with a view to a new Treaty.

14.3 EXTERNAL RELATIONS

1. Foreign relations falls within the second pillar of TEU.
2. Following ToA, the EU is represented in foreign affairs by the
Secretary-General to the Council.
3. Relations with the rest of the world can be strained,
particularly with the USA and the so-called 'tiger economies'
of the Far East, who are clearly unsympathetic towards a
trading area incorporating 350 million inhabitants and with
an agenda of continued enlargement.
4. Defence and security is also a difficult area internally because
of individual relationships, e.g. with NATO.

14.4 ECONOMIC AND MONETARY UNION

1. TEU set a timetable for entry into EMU in 1992.
2. There is now a common currency, the Euro, accepted by most
states – but this will not replace national currency until 2002.
3. States are, in any case, unable to participate until they meet
the 'convergence criteria'.
4. Sweden, the UK and Denmark are non-participants as yet.

5. Greece was originally ineligible, but has been eligible since 2001.
6. Denmark is unlikely to take part following a hostile national referendum.
7. The position of the UK is likely to be resolved during the lifetime of the current government.

Table of equivalent article numbering prior to the Treaty of Amsterdam

Previous Numbering	New Numbering
A2	A2
A3	A3
A3b	A5
A5	A10
A6	A12
A J.3 TEU	A13
A8	A17
A8a	A18
A8b	A19
A8c	A20
A8d	A21
A9	A23
A12	A25
A28	A26
A29	A27
A30	A28
A34	A29
A36	A30
A K.7 TEU	A35
A48	A39
A51	A42
A52	A43
A54	A44
A57	A47
159	A49
A60	A50
A66	A55
A85	A81
A86	A82
A90	A86
A95	A90
A100	A94

Previous Numbering	New Numbering
A100a	A95
A117	A136
A118	A137
A118A	A138
A118b	A139
A119	A141
A122	A145
A123	A146
A129a	A153
A137	A189
A142	A199
A145	A202
A148	A205
A151	A207
A155	A211
A157	A213
A158	A214
A164	A220
A169	A226
A170	A227
A173	A230
A175	A232
A176	A233
A177	A234
A188	A245
A189	A249
A198a	A263
A198c	A265
A215	A288
A235	A308
A238	A310

INDEX